YOU ASKED US

—

About Canada

THE ULTIMATE
FACT AND
TRIVIA BOOK

compiled by
Walter Stefaniuk

Doubleday Canada Limited

Canadian Cataloguing in Publication Data

Main entry under title:

You asked us — about Canada
Includes index.

ISBN 0-385-25578-0

1. Canada – Miscellanea. I. Stefaniuk, Walter.

FC61.Y68 1996   971'.002   C96-930563-X   F1008.3.Y68 1996

Cover design by Avril Orloff
Text design by Heidy Lawrance Associates
Printed and bound in Canada

Published in Canada by
Doubleday Canada Limited
105 Bond Street
Toronto, Ontario
M5B 1Y3

For Wes Ross, a teacher long dead now

CONTENTS

—

ACKNOWLEDGMENTS

Thousands of people had a hand in shaping this book, most of them readers of the *Toronto Star*'s You Asked Us column. Their questions dictated its contents and taught me this country's so-called identity crisis is a myth. Canadians know very well who they are, and are plenty proud of it, too. But they have an enormous curiosity about the country and the people who've built it over the past 500 years. I hope the following pages will help satisfy some of that curiosity.

Hundreds more generously provided the answers, many from their own experiences and knowledge. Others produced documents and statistics that couldn't be found in the usual places, encyclopedias, almanacs, newspaper files. They certainly made my work easy. Inevitably, mistakes will appear, but these are mine alone.

Scores of people at *The Toronto Star*, from copy editors to reporters, librarians to compositors, provided advice, encouragement, and have kept a protective eye over the column's progress.

But without tall Joe Hall, who liked the idea of a column based on reader input, and John Honderich, who suggested it include a question and answer segment, there'd have been no *You Asked Us*. Jim Foster took over the column when I was away and 18 of his nifty answers appear here. Peter Taylor showed me how a book is put together and guided it into the publishing world.

My family, headed by my wife, Jay, is large and supportive. But it was daughter Nicola who first suggested a book on the column's Canadian themes.

At Doubleday, editor Christine Innes whittled an oversized manuscript to manageable length so expertly I felt no pain.

Thank you all.

1

CANADA, FROM EH? TO ZED

Eh? is for accommodating
Why do Canadians say "eh?"

Because we're nice. Jack Chambers, professor of linguistics at the University of Toronto, a leading authority on Canadian dialects and expressions, explained: "What it is, the way Canadians use it, is a politeness marker. So when it comes up at the end of an assertion, it has a rising intonation, eH? And what the person who says it is trying to do is elicit your support — in general, include you in the conversation.

"It saves the person from making a bald assertion and instead allows the person to bring you in as a participant in the assertion. So it's a politeness marker. Canadians are, of course, renowned for being polite. Not rude, that is."

The fact is, he added, every other English-speaking nation uses eh in much the same way. "But the consensus is that Canadians use it more frequently, so it becomes associated with Canadians traditionally."

Eh's origin is obscure. It's one of the many hesitation markers in English. Every language has them. One that is common in the United States and other countries is huh. Hah? is another.

In French, *hein* functions in much the same way as eh, francophone friends advise. But it can be used in a sharply aggressive way, too. It's pronounced as a sort of nasal eh.

B is for Badlands
Were the Badlands named after western bandits who hid out there?
The name comes from the barren and rugged terrain itself, not from outlaws. It originated long before the arrival of the white man.

The Sioux called the rugged region of South Dakota *Mako Sika*, which means "Land Bad." French fur traders came along and called the eroded, dramatically sloped area of North Dakota and southern Alberta *les mauvaises terres*, which translates as bad lands.

The Badlands, which extend into southern Alberta along the Red Deer River Valley and to Saskatchewan, were formed by torrents in the wake of a retreating glacier between 10,000 and 15,000 years ago.

American outlaws found the Badlands a great hideout from pursuers though, according to history written in Hollywood.

C is for Canada, of course
How did Canada get its name?
It came borne on the wind.

The word "Canada" was first heard off Anticosti Island in the Gulf of St. Lawrence on August 13, 1535, during Jacques Cartier's second voyage of exploration.

Jesuit Pierre-Francois-Xavier de Charlevoix, the great early historian of New France, says it derived from the word "Kanata," a Huron-Iroquois term for village or community.

Two Indian youths Cartier had brought to France from his first voyage the previous year recognized familiar landmarks and pointed west across the waters, calling across the deck that this was the way to the *chemin de kanata* (route to the village). They were pointing in the direction of the St. Lawrence River, the route to the settlement of Stadacona.

Wooden sailing ships are noisy places. Timbers creak on the water, sails flap and rigging whines in the seabreezes. Even on an average day in August, land breezes at 13 km/h on the north shore of the Gulf are enough to extend light flags. Over open water, winds are stronger.

The boys' words reached Cartier's ears as *chemin de Canada* — road to Canada.

On August 17, Cartier noted his entrance to the great river: "The aforesaid Indians have assured us that this is the way to and the beginning of ... the route to Canada."

He later named the area controlled by Stadacona's chief, Donnacona, "the Province of Canada" and he called the St. Lawrence the "river of Canada." Stadacona was the site on which Quebec city would be built.

The name Canada first appeared on a map of the world about 1547, on land north of the great gulf and river. It became the popular name for the colony of New France among inhabitants, and in France, as well. Voltaire in his novel *Candide* and in his letters called the land Canada. He also called it "a few acres of snow."

But the British in the 13 colonies to the south usually referred to Canada after its capital, Quebec. Following the British conquest, the English name for the colony became the "Province of Quebec."

Many of the French inhabitants resisted the name Quebec. They preferred to be identified with the original name, Canada.

Eventually, the British succumbed and adopted the name Canada officially in the Canada Act of 1791, which divided the crown colony into Upper and Lower Canada. In the Act of Union in 1841, the two were reunited as the "British Province of Canada."

But, of course, given their celebrated Gaulish contrariness, the proud Canadiens at that point began to embrace the name Quebec for their beloved homeland.

When the British Colonies of North America discussed uniting, they needed a name for their new nation. There was Canada, the name of two of the colonies, of course. But the Fathers of

Confederation figured Queen Victoria would like Albertsland, to honor her late husband.

Among other names they considered: Albionara; Borealia; Britannia; Cabotia; Efisga, an acronym for England, France, Ireland, Scotland, Germany and Aboriginal lands (they overlooked Wales); Mesoplagia; Norland; Superior; Transatlantia, and Victorialand, after the Queen herself.

Fortunately, they discarded that whole list. At Confederation in 1867, the united colonies became the Dominion of Canada, 332 years after Cartier heard the name on the wind.

D is for Dominion
Why is Canada a Dominion?

The Fathers of Confederation wanted a Kingdom of Canada, but Britain's Foreign Office was nervous about the American reaction.

Sir Samuel Leonard Tilley, who read a chapter of the Bible every night, found a passage, the eighth verse of the 72nd Psalm: "He shall have dominion also from sea to sea, and from the river unto the ends of the earth." And that is how the new nation was designated in the British North America Act of 1867.

You don't see "Dominion of Canada" so often these days, but it's still our official designation under the Constitution Act of 1982.

E is for Down East
What's the difference between the Maritime provinces and the Atlantic provinces?

The Atlantic provinces include the Maritimes. Both terms were around in British North America before Confederation. Here's the history since 1867, from the Newfoundland and Labrador Geographical Names Board:

The term Maritime provinces refers to Canada's original three most easterly provinces. It was so widely used that the people of Nova Scotia, New Brunswick and Prince Edward Island (which entered Confederation in 1873), called themselves "Maritimers."

When Newfoundland joined Canada in 1949, the term Maritimes had for so long identified the three other provinces there was no real desire to change it. Atlantic provinces re-evolved as a way of accommodating Newfoundland's inclusion.

F is for the flag
What's the story behind Canada's flag? Who designed it?
George Stanley, a Calgary-born historian, educator and soldier, was dean of arts at the Royal Military College in Kingston when he submitted his maple leaf design during a nationwide search for a new flag in 1964.

Then prime minister Lester Pearson believed Canada needed a new flag as a symbol to unite its people, those of French and English ancestry and from everywhere else in the world.

It was a dangerous venture. Governments had retreated hastily from previous attempts, in 1925 and 1945, in the face of public opposition.

But the Pearson government held firm against concerted attacks from across the nation, led in Parliament by Opposition leader John Diefenbaker. Loyalist families and war veterans favored retention of the Red Ensign, a British merchant marine flag that had served unofficially as Canada's standard in peace and war since 1870.

Stanley's inspiration was the red and white commandant's flag that had flown from the military college's tower since 1900. In place of its armored-fist crest, Stanley copied the 11-point red maple leaf from the Canadian Coat of Arms.

"Regardless of the weather or the time of day, the red and white flag stood out, identifiable against the sky, against the gray of Kingston and the buildings of the Royal Military College," said Stanley, who also served as lieutenant-governor of New Brunswick.

Stanley believed that Canada's flag should be simplicity itself and in the traditional colors of Canada — which in heraldry and in history are red and white.

His design, one of more than 2,000 submitted, was officially adopted on December 15, 1965, after closure ended a long and bitter debate in Parliament.

The red and white Canadian Maple Leaf flag was officially raised for the first time over Parliament Hill at noon on February 15, 1965, and the maple leaf flew for the first time as Canada's chief symbol.

G is for the Greener card

Could I live in Canada but work in the United States for American dollars?

Yes, if you got a U.S. work permit — not the usual green card but a "commuter card."

If you made more than $10,000 (U.S.) a year you would have to pay U.S. income tax in those American dollars. Then you'd pay Canadian income tax in Canadian dollars, but deduct Washington's bite as a foreign tax credit. (Your Canadian tax bill would almost certainly be higher than the American one.)

It can get complicated. Revenue Canada has a toll-free number for advice from its international tax office: 1-800-267-5177.

H is for holidays

Do all provinces have their own special holiday such as Saint-Jean-Baptiste Day, now called *la Fête nationale* in Quebec?

The *Fête nationale* in Quebec falls every year on the saint's day, June 24, a legal holiday in the province since 1922. Most other provinces observe a civic holiday on the first Monday in August, but the name varies by province.

It's called the Civic Holiday in Manitoba, Saskatchewan, Northwest Territories and Ontario, but may have locally recognized names, such as Simcoe Day in the Toronto area.

The first Monday in August is called Heritage Day in Alberta. It's Natal Day, meaning birth day, in Prince Edward Island and most of Nova Scotia. Elsewhere, it's New Brunswick Day and British Columbia Day.

Newfoundland's civic holiday, Memorial Day, is celebrated on July 1. The Yukon's Discovery Day falls on the third Monday in August.

Alberta also has Family Day, the third Monday in February.

Also, the provinces and territories celebrate in common (though not all are statutory holidays): New Year's Day; Good Friday; Easter Sunday; Easter Monday; Victoria Day, which is also the official birthday in Canada of Queen Elizabeth II; Canada Day; Labor Day; Thanksgiving Day; Remembrance (Armistice) Day; Christmas Day; and Boxing Day.

I is for Indians
What's the origin of the term "Red Indians"? They're not, you know.
Probably from a misinterpretation in England of Anglo-Italian navigator John Cabot's description of natives he'd seen in 1497 who had painted their bodies red.

These were likely the now-extinct Beothuks of Newfoundland, known to have liberally adorned their bodies and possessions with a mixture of powdered hematite, red ochre.

Five years earlier, Christopher Columbus believed he'd reached India. He mistakenly called the Caribs he encountered Indians.

J is for Lynn Johnston's Canada
In Lynn Johnston's For Better or For Worse, Canadian place names are often mentioned. Characters have gone to London, Ont., Vancouver and Ottawa. Does the comic strip in the United States show Canadian landmarks and cities, or American stuff?
"Canadian stuff," said the folks at Universal Press Syndicate in Kansas City, Mo., which distributes the comic strip to more than 1,600 newspapers in the United States, Canada and the rest of the world.

They leave it the way Canadian cartoonist Lynn Johnston draws it.

"That was a stipulation I made," Johnston said when reached at her North Bay-area home.

To readers around the globe, the Canadian content is "for better."

"I put down Sault Ste. Marie once. I got letters from people who vacationed in Sault Ste. Marie, and I put down Vancouver and people from all over the place say, 'We've been there. We love it.' It's a very nice connection."

Johnston, who signed with Universal in September 1979, initially had to battle to keep the panel's Canadian place names. "At first, a couple of people at the syndicate were quite hostile about it."

But those people have long departed. And they were wrong about Canadian content hurting the comic strip in the U.S. marketplace or overseas in Europe, Japan, India. . . .

"It's been a plus, a big plus," the cartoonist said.

K isn't for "O Kanada"
Who wrote "O Canada" and how many bars did he lift from Mozart's opera "The Magic Flute"?

Adolphe-Basile Routhier wrote the words (in French) and Calixa Lavallée the music in Quebec City, probably in 1880. That was when it was first performed, anyway, as "Chant national."

It wasn't heard in English Canada for 20 years. Then it became a hit, and at least 25 anglicized versions are on record. The best-known English lyrics, by Robert Stanley Weir, were published in 1908.

Parliament approved it as our national anthem in 1967 and it was officially adopted June 27, 1980.

Now for the dirty stuff: Allegations of plagiarism in its opening passage were dismissed by Lavallée's biographer, Eugene Lapierre. He cited 13 composers besides Mozart who had used a similar sequence of notes.

Carl Morey, head of the Institute for Canadian Music, told us "maybe two bars" of the anthem's 28 bars have the same interval relation as a passage in the hymn for the priests in "The Magic Flute."

"It's a very common kind of pitch progression," he said. "The pattern appears countless times in 18th- and 19th-century music.

"I don't think Mozart would have sued."

L is for the loonie
What do they call the loonie in Quebec?

A popular nickname for the $1 coin is *pias*, which is what Quebecois used to call the $1 banknote. *Pias* is slang for *piastre*, a word for dollar descended from an old term for a coin. You can get by in Quebec calling it le dollar, though.

A voyageur, not a loon, was to appear on the $1 coin. But the voyageur lost its way in transit between Ottawa and the mint in Winnipeg. The loon die flew in as a substitute.

Derision greeted the heavy 11-sided coin of brass-plated nickle when introduced in July 1987. Canadians preferred the light convenience of the paper dollar, which never, ever rolled under sofas. The very idea of a $1 coin seemed loony. So, naturally, it became the loonie throughout English-speaking Canada.

In French-speaking Canada, it was first called *le huard*, a Quebecois term for a type of diving bird.

The term became so widely used that the Office de la langue française, the province's language watchdog, was moved to issue a press release saying, in effect: *Arret!* You have the wrong bird! It is more specifically and properly *un plongeon.*

Plongeon is the French word for loon and the bird on the $1 coin is, of course, a loon. But while Quebecers were willing to drop *le huard*, they weren't about to adopt the language office's *plongeon.* They compromised with *pias.*

Meanwhile, *plongeon* also means dive. Keep it in mind for those periods when the loonie plunges against the U.S. dollar.

M is for Marrow Bone
My English as a Second Language class located all but Marrowbone of the 23 place names mentioned in the Canadian

song, "Something to Sing About." Where is Marrowbone?

A hill called Marrow Bone — local usage is two words — is in the Torngat Mountains, on the northeastern edge of Labrador. It's northeast of Lake Melville, the closest large lake, say the folks at the Canadian Permanent Committee on Geographical Names, a branch of the government's National Atlas Information Service.

Labrador Inuit named the hill. The song was written by Canadian folksinger Oscar Brand in 1963.

Marrow Bone wasn't officially adopted as a Canadian placename until March 1980, which may be why the class couldn't find it in their reference material.

N is for No. 2
With the break-up of the Soviet Union, is Canada now the world's biggest country?

No. Canada's geographical area is 9,976,186 square kilometres (3.85 million square miles) and Russia alone, without its former 14 republics, is 17,075,272 square kilometres (6.59 million square miles).

That's about three-quarters the size of Canada, the U.S. and Mexico combined.

O is for the capital
Whatever possessed Queen Victoria to choose Ottawa as Canada's capital?

So bitterly did Toronto, Kingston, Montreal and Quebec City vie for the honor of becoming the capital of the new Province of Canada that the government feared it would be politically dangerous to choose any of them. The site for a permanent capital remained unsettled from the Act of Union in 1841 to 1857.

Officials then added unheralded Ottawa to the list and passed the hot potato on to Queen Victoria. They asked the monarch to arbitrate. She compromised by choosing Ottawa, then a lumber town of 10,000 people, incorporated as a city only two years before.

Canadian representatives apparently tipped the scales by whispering in the Queen's ear that Ottawa's location might be more defensible than its rivals in the event of hostilities with the U.S.

P is for the provinces
How did the provinces get their names?

Newfoundland was named by King Henry VII, who referred to John Cabot's discovery in 1497 as the "New Found Launde."

Nova Scotia is Latin for "New Scotland." The name was used in the royal charter that originally granted the land to Sir William Alexander in 1621. The charter was written in Latin.

Prince Edward Island was named in 1799 after a son of King George III, Prince Edward, commander-in-chief of British North America at the time.

New Brunswick was named in 1784 in honor of the reigning monarch, King George III, who was also Duke of Brunswick as a member of the German House of Hanover.

Quebec is derived from an Algonquin word for "narrow passage." It originally referred to the narrowing of the St. Lawrence River near what is now Quebec City. The British named the newly captured colony Quebec in 1763.

Ontario is of Indian origin, Huron words *onitari* for lake and *io* for beautiful. And *Kanadario* is Iroquoian for "sparkling water." The word Ontario appeared in 1641 to describe lands along the eastern Great Lakes and the name was applied to the province in 1867.

Manitoba comes from *Manitou bou*, which in Cree means "narrows of the Great Spirit" — named for where Lake Manitoba narrows at its center.

Saskatchewan is derived from the Cree name for the Saskatchewan River, *Ksiskatchewanisipi*, which means "swift-flowing river." Pioneers shortened it to Saskatchewan and in 1882 the name was given to the district, which, like Alberta, was then part of the Northwest Territories.

Alberta was named in honor of Queen Victoria's fourth daughter,

Princess Louise Caroline Alberta, in 1882. She was the wife of the Marquis of Lorne, governor general at the time.

British Columbia was known as New Caledonia in the north and Columbia in the south, after the Columbia River. To avoid confusion with Colombia in South America and the island of New Caledonia in the Pacific, Queen Victoria chose the name British Columbia for the colony in 1858.

The Northwest Territories were known as the North-Western Territory before 1870. Obviously, the name refers to the location.

Yukon comes from the Loucheaux Indian word for great river, *Yuchoo*. The Yukon River is the continent's fifth largest.

Q is for Her Majesty
When is the Queen's birthday? Where can I obtain her portrait? What's her address?
She was born April 21, 1926, in London. Her birthday is officially celebrated in Canada on the first Monday preceding the 25th of May — Victoria Day.

A photo of a formal portrait of Queen Elizabeth by Karsh can be had free of charge from the Governor General's headquarters in Ottawa. Write: Information Service, Rideau Hall, 1 Sussex Drive, Ottawa, Ont., K1A 0A1.

You may write to the Queen at: Her Majesty The Queen, Buckingham Palace, London SWI, England.

R is for now I remember
The motto on Quebec licence plates used to be *La belle province*. Now it's *Je me souviens* (I remember). Why? What do they remember?
The separatist Parti Quebecois replaced *La belle province* on licence plates with the Quebec motto, *Je me souviens*, in 1978.

Government bureaucrats polled in Quebec's transportion ministry, motor vehicle licence bureau and premier's office weren't sure. Somebody in the licence bureau thought it might refer to a societal memory of the glory of the Ancien Regime, before 1759 and all that.

Not quite. The full quotation from which the three sombre words were taken seems to bridge the two solitudes of Canada's founding peoples.

In French, it reads: *Je me souviens que né sous le lys, je crois sous la rose.*

The English translation is: "I remember that born under the lily, I grow under the rose."

Le lys is the fleur-de-lis, a symbol of the culture, language, laws and religion of Quebec since long before the Battle of the Plains of Abraham altered history in 1759; the rose is the rose of England under which the culture, language, civil law and religion of the old regime continued to flourish.

Architect Eugène Taché had the first three words inscribed beneath the coat of arms on the National Assembly building in Quebec City on February 9, 1883. The author is unknown.

S is for French Sault
What's the origin of the word Sault, as in Sault Ste. Marie?
Sault is French for rapids and the name, shared by neighboring Canadian and American cities, reflects French exploration, fur trade and settlement in the 1600s.

The two cities overlook rapids on the St. Mary's River, between Lakes Superior and Huron. Jesuits called their mission there Ste. Marie du Sault.

The Ojibwa name is *Bawating*, place by the rapids.

For what it's worth, French placenames — Pointe aux Pins, Pointe des Chenes, Gros Cap, Goulais, Desbarats — echo the past around the multicultural city on the Canadian side that has proclaimed itself officially unilingual, English-only.

Canadians aren't much for remembering their local traditions and history sometimes.

T is for Timiskaming, Temiskaming, Temiscamingue ...
Which is the correct spelling: Timiskaming or Temiskaming?
Oh, boy. Lake Timiskaming straddles the Ontario–Quebec border.
Temiscaming is the Quebec town at the southern end of lake. The
French spelling for the lake is Temiscamingue. On the Ontario side
is the District of Timiskaming.

Timiskaming is how it's spelled in the *Municipal Directory* published by the Ontario government, and on maps and various books
on place names.

Yet a lot of residents spell it Temiskaming. "There's been confusion over the spelling of the name for years," said Diane Beatty,
clerk-treasurer up in Haileybury when we called. She personally
preferred it with an "e." "That's the way I was taught and it's hard
to change."

Part of the confusion might be blamed on the post office. The
spelling of Timiskaming was changed to Temiskaming in post office
records on March 1, 1961, according to *Place Names of Ontario*,
which spells it Timiskaming. CPR records were also changed to
Temiskaming on that day.

However it's spelled, it's an Indian word meaning "place of deep,
dry water," referring to the clay flats in its northeastern part which
are dry when the water is low.

U is for Ungava far away
What does Ungava mean?
The name of the great peninsula and bay in northern Quebec means
"A far away place" in the language of Inuit there.

The old administrative district of Ungava was renamed New
Quebec after its transfer by the Government of Canada from the
Northwest Territories to the province in 1912.

V is for vivid names
**What was the original Indian name for the area we know as
British Columbia?**

None of the original inhabitants had a name for this immense geographical territory. But you could take your pick of haunting names for individual locales in seven separate Indian Language groups, such as Haida, Kwakiuti and Tsinshian, covering 32 different and distinct languages.

Here are a few examples of traditional place names in British Columbia, obtained from Peter McNair of the Royal British Columbia Museum in Victoria and in calls to various bands around the province:

North Vancouver, among the Squamish, is *Aslha'an*, which means "Up Against the Mountain."

To the Haida, the Queen Charlotte Islands are *Haida Gwaii*, "Territory of The People," *Haida* meaning "The People."

The Skeena band, near Hazelton in the interior, has a place called *Temiaham* (Eden). The Skeena River was traditionally known as *Ksan*, or "River of Mists," by the Gitksans who live along its banks. *Git* or *Kit* means "People."

Kitwancool is "People of the Narrow Place," for a location on a tributary flowing into the Skeena.

W is for wealth
Who controls most of the wealth in Canada?
The very rich of the Canadian establishment, but also many families who bought a house in a nice area in the 1960s or 1970s, have a good company pension plan and put a few dollars wisely aside, hitching onto growth in the economy and/or compound interest rates.

Wealth is more widely spread across the Canadian population than generally believed and much more evenly than in the United States and other countries, said Colin Deane, a principal with the accounting and consulting firm Ernst and Young, who headed up a study called *The Wealth Report*.

In the United States, the top 1 per cent of the population controlled 34.5 per cent of all personal assets in 1990.

But *The Wealth Report*, a year-long study released in 1990, found about 50 per cent of the wealth in Canada was controlled by families with total assets of $500,000 to $5 million, representing 11 per cent of all households.

Still, the very wealthy in Canada, those with assets of $5 million or more — about 0.2 per cent of the population — controlled a 12 per cent slice of the wealth.

It also determined that about 425,000 of 9.5 million households had net assets of more than $1 million.

An additional 4.4 million households were determined to have from $100,000 to $1 million in net assets. An additional 2.5 million families were in the $10,000 to $100,000 range. Households with under $10,000 in assets — including negative assets from business and consumer debts, mortgage to equity on real estate and so on — numbered about two million, four times the millionaire households.

The study, for banks and other financial institutions, remains the only major one of its kinds since Statistics Canada's 1983 Survey of Consumer Finances.

The Wealth Report found much of the wealth, particularly among the 425,000 millionaire families, came from home ownership at the outset of booming real estate cycles in the 1960s that continued through the '70s and much of the '80s.

"Most of those people would not consider themselves millionaires," Deane said.

A typical millionaire family in the Ernst and Young study might be an ordinary couple of about 55 or 60 who'd worked 20 years or more with a company with a pension plan (its value grown into the hundreds of thousands of dollars) and early on bought a house in a nice area — especially in Toronto or Vancouver. They'd likely have a bank account, RRSPs, perhaps a few other investments. Of course they'd have furnishings, collectibles, a car.

Aside from their money in bank and trust accounts, RRSPS and investments, most people tend to be unaware of or undervalue the worth of their home, company pension plans, and other assets, even the value of their businesses.

Only about 110,000 of these households had $1 million or more in investment assets, such as stocks, bonds, bank accounts — the classic gauge of the millionaire.

Average personal wealth varied in the different regions of Canada, from $395,000 in Ontario to $161,600 in Newfoundland.

The StatsCan Consumer Finances study, published in 1984, found that 5.1 per cent of Canadian families had a net worth in 1983 of $300,000 or more (about $450,000 today).

But proportions tend to become smaller as wealth increases, said Roger Love, chief of the Income and Expenditures section at Statistics Canada. He guesstimated the number of millionaires, based on 1983 findings, would total about 1 per cent of the population, 290,000 today.

StatsCan doesn't do studies to establish the precise number of individual millionaires simply because sample counts would be too small to be accurate. The census doesn't measure wealth aside from the value of the home, Love said.

The Ernst and Young study determined that between 1983 and 1990, the average Canadian family's financial worth had zoomed up by 125 per cent, largely from increases in value of homes owned for 20 years or more.

Despite a decline in property values between 1990 and 1995, the Canadian home remains a castle.

X is for the X-generation
What years were Baby Boomers born in, and when did Generation X come along?

The "Baby Boom" was the long period of soaring birth rate and prosperity after World War II, which began in 1946 in the U.S. and up to a year later in Canada. "Their troops came home a year before ours. They started having kids before we did," said economist David Foot of the University of Toronto, an authority on economic implications of changing demographics.

His data suggests the Canadian Baby Boom began in 1947 (other demographers say it started in 1946) and ended in 1966. Nevertheless, about nine million boomers are around.

Foot puts Generation X on the back quarter of the baby boom, from the peak in 1960 and edging into the 1970s. Now, on the Xers' heels, is the Baby Bust generation, young people born in the 1970s when fertility rates had plunged dramatically.

The Baby Boom grew over the 1950s and early 1960s with rising living standards "giving people more income to do everything, including·having kids."

Then the commercial introduction of birth control in the early '60s, plus rising wages for women, resulted in women of child-bearing age heading back into the labor force and dragged the fertility rate down, he said.

Enter Generation X, sometimes called the No-Name Generation or Lost Generation, now numbering about 2.25 million across Canada.

"The Generation X people really have had a tough life," Foot said. "Baby Boomers took all the jobs, drove up the value of everything they wanted to buy, like houses. Then (the Xers) suffered this whole early '80s recessionary phenomenon so they couldn't get their careers established. They entered the job market in the late 1970s, just in time for the recession of 1981-82 — "the last hired, first fired."

Even when recovery and growth extended through the mid-'80s, permanent jobs went to the younger people because they were cheaper and had updated technological skills, Foot said.

The prolonged recession in the early 1990s was their latest blow, one shared by the young Busters, who number perhaps 20 per cent of Generation X's population. Large numbers couldn't get jobs or their careers started, and continued to live with parents.

A study on young Metro families during the tail end of the 1990-92 recession underscored Foot's comments. Statistics of employable people showed jobs held by fewer than half those aged 15 to 24 and by only 74 per cent of those aged 25 to 34. The national jobless rate for all ages, boomers to busters, at that time of was just under 11 per cent.

Y is for Airports
Why is Pearson International Airport designated YYZ? Why do Canadian airports have a Y designation?

These are location identification codes — loc.IDs — used by commercial airlines for communications, timetables, tickets, baggage tags and so on.

In the early years of commercial aviation, cities — not airports — were given two-letter and three-letter codes.

Across the U.S., these were based on radio call signs of weather stations serving local airports. In those days, the call signs usually conformed to the name of the city.

But in Canada, two-letter designators developed by communications organizations were in use for transmitting weather reports long before commercial airline service flew into the picture.

Retired weather observers and telegraphers recall such station designators as VR for Vancouver, XE for Saskatoon, WG for Winnipeg, and YZ for Toronto.

The airlines picked up these established codes for their own communications and operational purposes.

An old American Aviation Traffic Guide shows the loc.ID for the airport serving Toronto in 1944 was the YZ designator and, to indicate inter-airline connecting flights, YYZ. The guide was pulled out by Marion Mistrik, librarian for the U.S. Air Transportation in Washington, D.C., to document what is mainly "oral history."

Location identification codes were finally approved for airports in 1945, at a meeting of national air transport associations in Washington, D.C. The letter Y was reserved to indicate Canadian airports and Z for its navigational aid stations.

Initially, two letters identified airports. Malton retained the Toronto weather station's original two-letter code, YZ. The City of Toronto became YT.

. With rapid post-war expansion of international air transport, the codes went to three letters. Malton, by then known as Toronto International Airport, was assigned another Y, becoming YYZ, the city's previous three-letter code for inter-airline traffic. Toronto itself went to YTO, Toronto Island Airport got YTZ, Buttonville YKZ and Hamilton YHM.

Designations that relate to the name of individual airports "are essentially the luck of the draw. They were available at the time," said Nathalie Thomas at the International Air Transport Association offices in Montreal. IATA administers the codes used worldwide by commercial airlines.

Designations for other major airports across Canada reflect old weather station designators: Goose Bay is YYR, Halifax is YHZ, Charlottetown YYG, Fredericton YFC, Saskatoon, YXE and Calgary YYC. Ottawa International is YOW, Winnipeg YWG, Edmonton YEG, Vancouver YVR. Montreal Dorval is YUL (the city's code used to be UL), and its sister airport, Mirabel International, built in the 1970s, is YMX.

Among foreign airports assigned loc.IDs in early pickings that got lucky: JFK for New York's John F. Kennedy, DFW for Dallas-Fort Worth, LAX for Los Angeles, LHR for London Heathrow and LGW for London Gatwick, MAN for Manchester International, ROM for Rome and HKG for Hong Kong.

But Chicago's O'Hare, the world's busiest airport is ORD, the code covering the original Orchard airport on the site.

Z is for O, Say can you Zee, eh?

About the letter Z, why do Americans say "zee" and Canadians say "zed"?

Zed is the elder way, related to the ancient Greek word Zeta. The Greeks used the names Alpha, Beta, etc. for their letters. Zeta is the sixth letter of their alphabet.

The Romans borrowed the Greek alphabet, but they didn't borrow the letters' Greek names, said linguist Henry Rogers of the

University of Toronto. The Romans used the sounds, ah, bay, etc.

They didn't need the letter Z but later adopted it anyway, mainly because it was useful for writing Greek words. They stuck Z way off at the end of the alphabet.

Many European languages have names for the letter that sound somewhat like Zeta, Rogers said. Zed is the English pronunciation.

That was the way it came to North America and that's the way it has remained in the Canadian pronunciation, though some Canadians have picked up the American way.

The Americans regularized Z to make it sound more like other letters of the alphabet, A, B, C, D, E ... Zee.

2

SEA TO SEA AND BACK AGAIN

Center of Canada

Geographically speaking, where is the center of Canada?

It's near Arviat, N.W.T., on the west coast of Hudson Bay. If you have an older map, look for Eskimo Point. That's what Arviat (pop. 1,100) used to be called. The co-ordinates are 60 degrees 6 minutes and 30 minutes of latitude north and 94 degrees 3 minutes and 30 seconds longtitude west.

But with the irregular shape of the country, that's a subjective reckoning, said Susan Blackie of the Geodetic Survey Division of Geomatics Canada. Arviat is at the intersection of lines between Canada's most northerly and southerly points and most easterly and westerly points, adjusted for other factors, such as land mass.

She recalled how a researcher once traced an outline of a map of Canada on a sheet of metal, cut it out and lightheartedly determined the centre by balancing the metal on pin. It was near Arviat.

If you're for the point midway on the great circle from, say, St. John's, Nfld., 5,078 kilometres to Victoria, B.C., it's smack in the middle of Northern Ontario, just north of the Winisk River Waterway Provincial Park.

Half-time in Newfoundland
Why is Newfoundland in a time zone that is on a half-hour?
Time zones coincide with even multiples of 15 degrees longitude, the distance the sun appears to travel every hour, from the meridian through Greenwich, England — 15 degrees, 30 degrees, 45 degrees and so on.

The bulk of Newfoundland's population lies virtually between two time zones. Instead of opting for one or the other, they split the difference, said Paul Delaney of York University's physics and astronomy department.

Clocks in Canada are set in six time zones. Newfoundland time is centered on 52½ degrees west, near St. John's, minus 3½ hours (as the sun travels) from Greenwich. If it's 12:30 p.m. in Newfoundland, it's 12 noon in the Maritimes, 11 a.m. in Quebec and Ontario, 10 a.m. in Manitoba and Saskatchewan, 9 a.m. in Alberta and 8 a.m. in British Columbia and Yukon Territory.

The Ontario-Quebec time zone is centered at 75 degrees west, near Cornwall, minus five hours from Greenwich.

Deal of a century
What was the name of the sugar island for which France gave up Canada in negotiations with Britain, and what was the date?
France regained the tiny Caribbean islands of Guadeloupe and Martinique from Britain and gave up Canada in the 1763 Treaty of Paris. France tossed in Grenada and the Grenadines to sweeten the deal.

France retained fishing rights in Newfoundland waters and the islands of St. Pierre and Miquelon, kept its trading stations in India and a couple of other spots on the globe under terms of the treaty that ended the North American end of Europe's Seven Years War.

In return, Britain got Canada, much as it is today, France's territories east of the Mississippi River (aside from Louisiana which went to France's ally, Spain) and Florida from Spain.

The treaty, signed February 10, 1763, confirmed the supremacy of Britain as a colonial and maritime power, a supremacy it maintained for most of two centuries. As for France, it had already dismissed Canada, in the words of the great Voltaire, as "a few acres of snow," later adding, "by losing Canada, you lose nothing."

Days of sail and steam
How many days did it take early steamships to cross the Atlantic? Was it faster than sail? How long would it take to sail from London to Quebec City in the summer of 1832?

The first steam-powered vessel to cross the Atlantic was the American paddlewheeler Savannah in 1819. That took 29 days, but only 85 hours was under steam before it ran out of coal and wood. The rest of the trip from New York to Liverpool was under sail.

In 1833, Samuel Cunard's paddlewheeler Royal William crossed from Halifax to Bristol in 25 days, mostly under steam. But the first ship to cross under steam power alone was the British Sirius in 1838. That took 18½ days, and the days of sailing ships in commerce were numbered.

"A good sail would probably take four to five weeks, sometimes longer," says Edward Laine, a historian at the Canadian Museum of Civilization in Hull, Que. "There were certain variables, of course — the season, the weather, winds, currents and knowledge of these, as well."

The trip to Quebec City could have been done in four more days, but Laine added that "scows they had were not designed for speed, but to carry cargo."

Clipper ships could outrun the early steamers, but they were used in the tea trade from the Orient rather than the North Atlantic run. One clipper was reputed to sail as fast as 20 knots, "which would put it in the range of late 19th-century propeller-driven ships (a Canadian invention) rather than paddlewheelers," Laine said.

Other sailing ships of the 1830s might do nine or ten knots, if they were going well. Steamers would do that and perhaps a bit more. "Of course, they had the advantage they didn't have to tack into the wind."

A dry Niagara Falls
Was Niagara Falls ever turned off?
The mighty Niagara River ran dry March 30, 1848, and stayed dry for 30 hours. "The sudden silence startled hundreds from their sleep and filled churches with those who feared the end of the world," according to Environment Canada's Weather Calendar.

While a massive ice jam plugged a narrow stretch near Buffalo, daredevils strolled across the river bed. A miller named Samuel Street planted a flag on the lip of Canada's Horseshoe Falls. Eventually tonnes of ice shook free with a warning rumble, folks rushed ashore and the falls turned on again.

Despite upstream power stations, man hasn't tampered much with the Canadian falls, which get 90 per cent of the river's flow. In 1954-55 a cleanup at the edge temporarily diverted more water to the American cascade, but not enough to spoil the main attraction.

However, the Americans pulled the plug on their falls in 1969. A temporary dam between the riverbank and Squaw Island reduced the rapids to a drip while geologists and engineers studied rock-falls that have gradually diminished the American spectacle. Three remedial plans were considered, but nothing was done.

St. John's settled in 1500s
Which is the oldest city, Quebec City, St. John's, or St. Augustine?
St. Augustine in Florida, founded by Spaniards in 1565, is considered the oldest city in the United States.

Quebec City dates to 1608 when Samuel de Champlain built a fort at the site of an ancient Iroquoian settlement of Stadacona, which Jacques Cartier had visited in 1535.

For St. John's, Nfld., whose 500th anniversary of the visit by discoverer John Cabot is 1997, it all depends on how you define oldest. "If it's oldest settlement, we've got the other cities beat," said St. John's archivist Helen Miller.

"In the early 1500s, the first settlers came, but under British law, no settlement was allowed — in theory — until the 1700s," she said.

European fishermen had followed quickly in Cabot's wake, and set up fishing stations and huts around the harbor. By the time Sir Humphrey Gilbert landed in 1583 to formally claim the territory, two fishing settlements were thriving on the harbor's north shore.

But if the criteria is formal municipal status, St. John's is a latecomer. Though the island's capital and biggest town, it was run by a Newfoundland government department till 1888.

As for the oldest city in North America, an Aztec capital established in 1325 had a population of about 500,000 when the Spaniard Hernando Cortes razed it in 1521 and established Mexico City on its ruins.

Logan stands tall
What's Canada's highest mountain? Is it world-class?
Mount Logan in the Yukon rises to 5,951 metres, second in North America only to Alaska's Mount McKinley at 6,190 metres. As for its standing in the world, Logan is higher than any mountain in Europe, Africa, Antarctica or Oceania. Asia's Himalayas and South America's Andes have peaks far higher.

Oldest rocks in the world
How old is the Canadian Shield? Are these low mountains really the oldest in the world?
The oldest known rock of this planet — 3.96 billion years — is in the Canadian Shield north of Yellowknife in the N.W.T. Rocks up to 3.9 billion years old have been found halfway up the Labrador coast, near Nain. Rock 3.6 billion years old has also been found in northernmost Quebec.

"It's an accident of nature that these rocks even survived," said research scientist Randall Parrish, who heads the geochronology lab of the Geological Survey of Canada.

In general, most of the rock of today's Canadian Shield formed during two mountain-building periods, about 2.7 billion and 1.8

billion years ago — the latter being the coming together of the continent as we know it, Parrish said.

The shield of crystalline rocks runs in a great arc north and east of the biggest lakes in Canada from Inuvik, near the Beaufort Sea, down through northern Saskatchewan, Manitoba, Ontario (running north of Toronto) and on to the St. Lawrence River and up into Labrador. Its age is dated by chemical analysis of radioactive decay.

Elsewhere, belts of rock that might predate 2.7 billion years have been found in parts of South Africa, Australia and the Antarctic. "They look like hills now — just like they do up near Wawa — but they also are the roots of much larger mountains," Parrish said.

The Grenville mountain system, extending along the southeastern edge of the Canadian Shield from Labrador through Kingston and Peterborough to Georgian Bay, is about one billion years old, and "represents one big continental plate that bashed against another," he said.

The Appalachians, including the Canadian Maritimes, go back 550 million years — teenagers in the Earth's geological time. The Rockies became an important mountain system about 135 million years ago. The Alps and Himalayas, which began forming about 40 million years ago, are babies compared to the age of the Canadian Shield.

To what height the shield's ancient mountains towered eons ago is unknown, but Parrish suggested they were likely between the size of the Himalayas — "which is probably as big as mountains get" — and the Alps.

Land of volcanoes
Does Canada have any volcanoes? If so, where?
Canada has hundreds of volcanoes of virtually every type known on Earth, from small cinder cones to giants with the potential explosive power of Washington's Mount St. Helens or the Philippines' Mount Pinatubo.

But people east of the Rockies don't have to worry too much, said volcanologist Catherine Hickson of the Geological Survey of Canada, based in Vancouver. Only traces of volcanoes remain in the rest of Canada from belts that existed during collisions of continents hundreds of millions and billions of years ago.

Geologically young volcanoes are found in the Coastal Mountains of British Columbia and into the Yukon, along the "Ring of Fire," the volcano and earthquake belt that girdles the Pacific Ocean.

Canada has volcanoes bigger than Mount St. Helens, Hickson said. St. Helens was the 2,549-metre peak in the Cascades Range, 150 kilometres south of Seattle, until it blew off 300 metres of its top in an 1980 eruption that killed 57 people.

One of the Canadian volcanoes watched most closely is Mount Meager, 100 kilometres north of Vancouver. The name doesn't come from its size — it towers 2,645 metres — but from a J.B. Meager, who held early timber rights there.

"It last erupted 2,400 years ago. That eruption was bigger than the 1980 eruption of Mount St. Helens," Hickson said. "We know that from what was spewed by the volcanic eruption. We can trace ash from that eruption into Alberta."

Eruptions differ in kinds of magma (melted rock) expelled. Mount Meager is of the explosive dacite type, like St. Helens and Pinatubo, whose 1991 emissions are believed to have disrupted world weather.

Between Meager and Vancouver are Mounts Garibaldi and Caley, both active during the last two million years.

If Canada's volcanoes aren't famous, it's because they're mostly in remote areas and have been silent lately. The last eruption occurred more than a century ago, reported by gold miners in northwestern B.C. Another occurred more than 150 years ago near what is now Terrace, B.C. Precise dating is hampered by lack of witness accounts.

Three types of stresses create the Canadian volcanoes. In the Garibaldi belt, which sweeps north from the Cascades, and the Yukon's Wrangell belt, ocean plates burrow under the continental plate. In the Stikine belt in northwestern B.C., plates are moving in different directions. "Hot spot" volcanoes stem from molten material seeping up through solid crust, as in the Anahim belt, northwest of the Garibaldis.

But aside from Mount Meager, the most recently active volcano near populated areas is 1,800-metre Mount Baker, in the State of Washington, which Hickson can see from her office window.

Big land, big waters
Does Canada have more water than land?
No, not even if you take in the salt water within Canada's territorial limits off shore.

Just about any world encyclopedia or world almanac will tell you Canada is the second largest country in the world — after Russia — with a land area of approximately 9.2 million square kilometres (9,221,006, to be precise), and a fresh water area of 755,180 square kilometres.

But in addition, there's about 6,650,000 square kilometres of salt water on Canada's "continental margin," said Claire Gosson, geographer at the National Atlas Information Service in Ottawa. "That is about two-thirds the land area, the second largest continental margin in the world" (after Russia), she said.

The Beaufort Sea, Canadian Arctic Archipelgao, including Baffin Bay and Davis Strait, extend over about three million square kilometres. James Bay, Hudson Bay and Hudson Strait cover one million square kilometres; the east coast covers 2.5 million square kilometres, and the west coast 150,000 square kilometres.

100 miles from Lillooet
What's the significance of mileage in the name 100 Mile House in British Columbia? Looking at my map I also see 70 Mile House and 108 Mile House.
Those are distances from Mile 0 at Lillooet, B.C., along the old Cariboo Wagon Road. House meant a trading post or store where

travellers could obtain supplies and fresh horses in the wilderness.

Settlement of 100 Mile House, about 450 kilometres northeast of Vancouver, began about 1862, a natural stop on the trail during the Cariboo Gold Rush centered on Barkerville, an arduous 200 miles (320 kilometres) further along. The village of 1,800 remains a popular stop for motorists whizzing along the modern Cariboo Trail.

In Ontario, a number of creeks are also named for mileage. For example, 16 Mile Creek through Oakville gets its name because its mouth is 16 miles from the starting point of an early survey along Lake Ontario. It appeared as Sixteen Mile Creek on an 1800 map.

Yonge, world's longest street
Yonge St. is supposed to be the longest street in the world. Who lives in the last house along its route?
Yonge St., better known as Highway 11 along most of its route from Toronto to the international border at Rainy River, is in record books as the world's longest street.

That's as far as you can go on extensions to the original road begun in 1795 by Lieutenant-Governor John Graves Simcoe, who named it after a friend, Sir George Yonge, British secretary of state for war.

The original Yonge St. was completed in 1796, from Queen St. 54 kilometres of mud and tree stumps north to Holland Landing.

Today, the provincial highway starts at Toronto's waterfront at One Yonge St. and runs 1,882.3 kilometres (1,170 miles), up past Lake Simcoe, an early destination, through Muskoka to North Bay, Kapuskasing, Hearst, Thunder Bay, Fort Frances and into Rainy River. The last house, siding on the road, belongs to Alex Warnuk, a retired customs officer.

But the fact is, once it passes Newmarket just north of Toronto, fewer and fewer people call it Yonge St. The name is soon left behind as the kilometres roll and its identity becomes Highway 11. Occasionally, it assumes other aliases as it passes through communities along its way. In Rainy River it ends as Attwood Ave. W.

The last four blocks of the provincial highway are a mix of commercial buildings and vacant lots. The very last building is Canada Customs at the Baudette-Rainy River International Bridge. "Come on up and see us," said customs officer Vern Good, who was on duty when we called. Next door is an oil company distributorship. At the bridge, Ontario Highway 11, Yonge St., officially ends.

Highway mileage
When you see a sign on the highway, "Thunder Bay 96 kilometres," what is the point they measured?
Mileage signs are measured from the city center out.

New Caledonia
Which Canadian province was once called New Caledonia?
New Caledonia was to be the name of the new crown colony established in 1858 on the Pacific side of British North America. But a French possession in the south seas already had that name. To avoid confusion, Queen Victoria opted to call the colony British Columbia.

A half-century earlier, explorer and fur trader Simon Fraser named the territory's central highlands region New Caledonia — New Scotland — because he imagined the mountains and valleys were like the Scottish Highlands as described by his mother.

By British Columbia's entry into Confederation in 1871, New Caledonia had disappeared from use.

Nahanni far away
How were the Nahanni Rivers in the Northwest Territories named?
For the aboriginal people living in the area in the 1800s. Today, however, authorities feel there was no distinct Nahanni (Nahani, Nahane, Nahennie) tribe. It's an Athapaskan word translated as "people of the west" or "people over there far away."

Cap'n Davis
For whom was the Davis Strait, between Greenland and Baffin Island, named?

The strait was named for English navigator John Davis, sometimes written Davys (born about 1550), an Elizabethan sea captain, marine writer, inventor and one of the great Arctic explorers. He mounted three voyages to seek the Northwest Passage.

His *Seaman's Secrets* became a sailor's handbook. His accounts of Inuit are considered among the most accurate and sympathetic of early observations. Elizabethans admired him for his courage and character. Davis was killed in 1605, by Japanese pirates off Malaysia during a voyage for the East Indies Co.

Saltwater and tides
Are Hudson Bay and James Bay freshwater?

Salt water. "We get tides up here, as well," said Constable Eric Cheechoo of Moose Factory First Nation Reserve Police, located at the mouth of the Moose River on James Bay.

Great seas in their own right, both were discovered by Henry Hudson. James Bay is named for navigator Thomas James, who sailed into it in 1631.

Lake of the Slavey
Why did Great Slave Lake get that name?

English explorer Samuel Hearne, who in 1771 became the first European to reach the lake, named it after the Slavey (or Slave) Indians. Yellowknife, capital of the Northwest Territories, is on a northern arm of the lake, the continent's fifth largest.

A trail of two subways
How many kilometres of subway lines are there in Toronto?
How many kilometres of subway lines are there in Montreal?

Metro Toronto has about 57 kilometres (35 miles) of subways. These run along two routes, the Yonge-University-Spadina great "U" and the Bloor-Danforth line. Along the way in the Toronto Transit Commission system are 65 subway stations.

Montreal's "Metro" runs 65 kilometres and has 65 stations on four subway lines. The folks at the Metro say these are easily identified by color coding as the Green, Orange, Yellow and Blue lines.

Metro Toronto has provincial backing for 6.4 kilometres (4 miles) of new line along Sheppard Avenue. On hold is 4.8 kilometres (3 miles) of an Eglinton West line. In the future is a 5.1-kilometre (3.2-mile) extension of the Spadina line to York University.

In Montreal, no subway extension is in the works aside from a feasibility study for a North Shore line to Laval.

Land's end
What does the name Gaspé mean?
It's the French spelling of a Mic Mac word for "land's end."

Due north
Where does southern Ontario end and Northern Ontario begin?
The line is the southern boundary of Parry Sound district. Northern Ontario is made up of the Territorial Districts of Algoma, Cochrane, Kenora, Manitoulin, Nippising, Parry Sound, Rainy River, Sudbury, Timiskaming and Thunder Bay. That's the provincial transportation ministry's definition, outlining Northern Ontario for purposes of exempting residents from vehicle licence fees.

Park over century old
What is the area of Algonquin Park and when was it established?
The 7,600-square-kilometre (2,935 square-mile) provincial park, spread between Huntsville and Pembroke, was established in 1893 and is Ontario's oldest.

Gooseville
What does Wawa mean?

Wild goose. It comes from Ojibwa, the language of the people there long before fur traders came in the 17th century.

To many travellers along the Trans-Canada Highway as it arcs along the north shore of lake Superior, Wawa's a rest stop, a mining town — gold from about the turn of the 20th century and iron ore today — 240 kilometres northwest of Sault Ste. Marie.

Alaska boundary dispute
Why does the coast of Alaska go so far down into what you'd expect to be the coast of British Columbia?

Creation of the 640-kilometre-long panhandle goes back to British colonial times, long before the U.S. purchased Alaska from Russia for $7.2 million (U.S.) in 1867. Russia claimed the coast to the 51st parallel by right of exploration, trading and fishing.

In an 1825 treaty with Britain, Russia got the coastline south to latitude 54 degrees 40 minutes, to a distance ten marine miles inland, as its southern boundary in North America, and Britain was given navigation of streams crossing Russian territory. But so indefinite was the language of the treaty that Russia and Britain went away with different impressions of where the boundary actually ran.

Here's the contentious clause, in Article IV of the treaty: "That whenever the summit of the mountains which extend in a direction parallel to the coast, from the 56th degree of north latitude to the point of intersection of the 141st degree of west longitude, shall prove to be at the distance of more than 10 marine leagues from the ocean, the limit between the British possessions and the line of the coast which is to belong to Russia, as above mentioned, shall be formed by a line parallel to the winding of the coast, and which shall never exceed the distance of 10 marine leagues therefrom."

After the U.S. purchased Alaska, it maintained the ten miles inland included the distance from the heads of coastal fiords, which extended deep into the interior — for a panhandle ten miles to 150 miles (242 kilometres) wide.

Canadians strongly disputed that interpretation. The boundary issue came to a head after the Klondike gold rush began in the spring of 1897 when tens of thousands of prospectors had to cross land claimed by the U.S. to reach the Yukon from North Pacific waters.

Three Americans and two Canadian representatives on a tribunal in London to settle the boundary dispute in 1903 held to partisan positions. The Americans wanted an unbroken boundary and the Canadians stated the boundary should cut across inlets and fiords. The sixth member, Lord Alverstone, Lord Chief Justice of England, sided with the U.S. This helped warm British-U.S. relations after 125 years of mistrust.

But the decision created anti-British sentiment in Canada and momentum for full independence. Britain then was still running Canada's foreign policy and boundary negotiations. The boundary decision was one of the reasons for the creation of a small Department of External Affairs in 1909 and rejection of free trade with the U.S. in the 1911 election.

3

THE C WORD – CONSTITUTION

Treason and the separatists

What constitutes treason in Canada? Why weren't separatist MPs charged with treason? Isn't working for secession treason? Speaking and acting openly and peacefully for the break-up of Canada isn't treason. Freedom of speech is one of their four most basic rights as Canadians. Freedom of citizens to seek political change is the strength and the fragility of great democracies.

In the evolution of democracies, yesterday's traitor may be tomorrow's hero. The hanged Louis Riel is now recognized as one of the heroes of Canada, hailed as a visionary and patriot.

Treason is one of the oldest crimes described in law, originally a crime against the monarch. It still is. Under the Criminal Code of Canada, "high treason" is harming or attempting to harm the Queen and inciting rebellion.

Treason is committed by anyone who uses force or violence in an attempt to overthrow the federal or a provincial government, or who unlawfully gives a foreign agent information that may prejudice the safety or defence of Canada. Conspiracy to commit any of these is also treason.

Spying is also covered under the Official Secrets Act. "But it is not treasonous to work through democratic means for the break-up of Canada," said political scientist Peter Russell of the University of Toronto, an authority on such questions. "Many, many prominent Canadians have done so since the separatist movement began. There's nothing treasonous about that as long as it's not done secretly or through force of arms."

Russell served as research director for the McDonald Royal Commission into the Royal Canadian Mounted Police's handling of potential insurrection in Quebec in the 1970s, one of the most intensive and expensive investigations in Canadian history.

Some texts suggest it would be treasonous for a province to secede without Parliament's approval. Russell disagreed: "If a province just decided to separate, without amendment to the Constitution, it would be illegal and unconstitutional, but not treason. It would be a breach of the Canadian Constitution if not negotiated within the Constitution. But you could amend the Constitution to eliminate the province (changing such clauses as those referring to representation by provinces in the Commons and Senate)."

Lawyer Robert Lemieux, who defended FLQ members after the 1970 October Crisis, said none was accused of treason but many, including himself, were charged with sedition. That's a sort of second-cousin to treason and basically means stirring up discontent or rebellion.

An incident the day of the 1995 Quebec referendum on separation in which a Bloc Quebecois member urged francophone members of the Canadian Forces to "transfer their loyalty to the new country" was seen by many as sedition under Section 62 (1) of the Criminal Code of Canada, but not treason. The federal government did not pursue the matter.

Lemieux suggested that statements some anglophones deem treasonous are simply legal or historical facts. An example is the separatist argument that Quebec wouldn't necessarily require Parliament's permission to secede. A case could be made that the 1841 Act of Union that joined the independent colony of Quebec with

Ontario into the Province of Canada was arbitrary and "wasn't a democratic act," he said.

Quebec, which technically came into being in 1608 with the founding of the village of Quebec, has been independent longer than it's been federated, he said. To utter a historical fact is not treasonous.

Canada's most famous and tragic treason case was that of Riel, who was found guilty and hanged in 1885 after leading Métis and Indian uprisings in the West. Today, he's generally recognized as a great patriot, a protector of Métis and Indian rights and, to admirers, the Métis' Father of Confederation.

Treason and other crimes against the state are some of the most serious offences in criminal law, though "rarely committed and still more rarely charged," the Law Reform Commission of Canada said in a 1988 report. It did not touch on secession.

Freedoms in Canada

In the 1940s, the government advertised five freedoms. I believe two were freedom of speech and freedom of thought. I can't find any information on the other freedoms. What are they?

Four freedoms — freedom of speech and expression, freedom of religion, freedom from want and freedom from fear (of aggressors) — were proclaimed on January 6, 1941, by American president Franklin D. Roosevelt as basic rights the United States would defend anywhere in the world.

Roosevelt was attempting to win congressional support for a lend-lease program to provide materials to countries fighting for survival against the Axis powers.

The four freedoms were hailed as basic tenets of modern civilization and, in 1948, the United Nations adopted the Universal Declaration of Human Rights, which included 30 articles defining civil, political, economic, social and cultural rights and freedoms.

In Canada, the 1982 Charter of Rights and Freedoms also guarantees four fundamental freedoms: of conscience and religion; of thought, belief, opinion and expression, including freedom of the press; of peaceful assembly; of association.

It also guarantees democratic, mobility, legal, and equality rights.

In line for the top
What is the chain of command in the American and Canadian political system? The vice-president would become acting president of the United States if the president is incapacitated, but who'd follow the veep?

In the U.S. order of succession: the vice-president; speaker of the House of Representatives; president pro tempore of the Senate; then cabinet members in order of historic rank: the secretary of state, treasury, defence, the attorney-general, the secretary of the interior, agriculture, commerce, labor, health, housing, transportation, energy and education.

If a president dies, resigns or is removed from office, the vice-president is sworn in as president and nominates a new vice-president who takes office after being confirmed by Congress.

No laws cover such circumstances in Canada, only the generalities of British parliamentary tradition. The governor general, as representative of the Queen, would appoint a new prime minister after hearing the advice of the government — the cabinet and caucus of the party in power.

Gee Gee's role
What does the governor general do and what's the cost?

Parliament's three elements are the Commons, the Senate and the Queen.

As her representative, the governor general — on recommendation of the government — summons, prorogues and dissolves Parliament, gives royal assent to bills, appoints Senators and superior court judges in all provinces, signs treaties, receives and sends ambassadors, and appoints as Prime Minister the leader of the majority in Parliament.

Among other duties and responsibilities, the governor general is keeper of the nation's honors and awards, the nation's host to visiting heads of state, and the commander-in-chief of Canadian Forces.

Though the office is largely ceremonial and above politics (the governor general used to be an agent of the British Government), the governor general continues to hold certain prerogative powers for the crown on behalf of the people. These are designed as a check should a government flagrantly abuse constitutional propriety.

The governor general could dismiss a government and order an election. It's never happened at the federal level, but in 1926, Viscount Byng refused Prime Minister Mackenzie King's request to dissolve Parliament for an election and asked Arthur Meighen to form a government.

The cost to the public purse is a $97,375 a year tax-free salary and an annual budget of just over $10 million, not including about $2 million for upkeep of historic residences, Rideau Hall in Ottawa and The Citadel in Quebec City.

Under a republican system, such costs are for presidential heads of state.

The office spans almost four centuries of Canadian history. The line of vice-regal representatives in Canada goes back years to the "Father of New France," Samuel de Champlain. Romeo LeBlanc of New Brunswick is the 62nd person since 1627 appointed to that office — through the French and British regimes and since Confederation.

Finally, the Constitution doesn't cover the break-up of Canada. Although opinion is sharply divided on the amending formula, experts believe negotiations for separation or for reshaping the nation must consider the constitutional powers of the governor general. Changes to the Constitution affecting the governor general would require unanimous consent of the federal government and ten provinces or at least seven provinces representing 50 per cent of the population.

In this way, the governor general as representative of the monarch is one of the ties that help bind the provinces into a nation.

Choosing a Prime Minister
How can 3,500 people at a political convention pick a new prime minister, as happened with Kim Campbell in 1993? That should be left up to the people of Canada in an election.
In fact, it is the governor general who selects the new prime minister and cabinet ministers, acting on behalf of the sovereign.

Delegates at a federal party's leadership convention merely choose a new political leader for the party in Parliament. If the party has the majority of seats in the House of Commons and forms the government, the new leader undoubtedly will become Canada's next prime minister.

Here is the ritual in the transfer of power to a new prime minister in such cases, honed in Canadian political tradition since 1867 and evolved over centuries of British history.

The prime minister visits the governor general to advise of the results of the leadership convention. The PM announces the party has unanimously — based on the runner-up's traditional motion of unanimity — chosen a new leader. The prime minister then informs the G G that, as already indicated, he or she will be resigning.

The governor general will wait a day or two, "a delicate pause," ostensibly to determine which party holds the most seats in the House of Commons and consider the circumstances, before summoning the new leader to Rideau Hall to invite her or him to try to form a government.

A few days later, anywhere from seven days to a fortnight from the convention — the mechanics of transition take time — the new leader returns to Rideau Hall to announce that, yep, a government can be formed. Together they formally set the date for the official transfer of power (which will coincide with that already set by the transition team, of course).

The same ritual holds when a government has been defeated at the polls. The defeated prime minister arrives to apprise the GG of the election results and announces the intention to resign. The Opposition Leader whose party has garnered the most seats is summoned and invited to try and form a government. The new leader returns in a couple of days to announce that, yes, a government can be formed and a formal date is agreed upon for the transfer of power).

On that date, at the appointed hour, the outgoing prime minister arrives at Rideau Hall accompanied by the registrar-general, who carries the Great Seal of Canada, the symbol of government authority. This is given to the governor general. The Prime Minister hands over the letter resigning office and cabinet.

For the next hour or so, Canada is without a prime minister and cabinet. The sole responsibility and authority for governing lies with the governor general. That's why the monarch's representative is in possession of the Great Seal.

Meanwhile, the prime minister-designate and cabinet appointees are each making their way to Rideau Hall for the swearing-in ceremony.

The leader is the first to take the oath of office. When this is done, the new prime minister signs an instrument of advice to the governor general, which is in effect the list of cabinet appointees. The governor general also signs it, indicating agreement, and its members are sworn in.

The Great Seal is then given to the new registrar-general. The ritual is ended, and the new prime minister and cabinet sent off to govern.

Length of government

How long can a Canadian government stay in power. Five years?
A government could choose to remain in power for almost six years, though Parliament itself automatically would be dissolved at the end of its five-year mandate, the maximum allowed under the Constitution.

The Constitution says no House of Commons shall continue for longer than five years from the date fixed for the return of the writs from the previous election.

But, theoretically, a government can stay in power beyond the five years if it chooses, without a Parliament behind it. It's possible to obtain money by means of governor general's warrants and pass directives through orders-in-council.

There's even a precedent in this country: Conservatives governed without an election from 1911 to 1917 during World War I.

The 1982 Constitution provides that Parliament must sit at least once every 12 months. And one of the things that does is put a time limit on how long a government may cling to power. This means within 12 months after the dissolution of the old Parliament, a newly elected Parliament, sworn-in government and all, must be installed.

Canadian governments traditionally have called elections well before the House of Commons' five-year mandate expires.

Canadian franchise
Who is eligible to vote in federal elections?

You have to be a citizen of Canada and at least 18 years old on voting day. You must also be resident in Canada on the first day of enumeration, which is 38 days before the election.

4

LAW AND ORDER

Death penalty in Canada
When was capital punishment abolished in Canada?
The death penalty remains on the books under the National Defence Act for 32 offences involving cowardice, desertion, unlawful surrender and treachery, spying for the enemy and for mutiny accompanied by violence.

But it was lifted from the Criminal Code (except for killers of police and prison guards, initially), for five-year periods after narrow votes in the House of Commons in 1967 and 1973. Executions under the Code were abolished altogether on July 14, 1976. Attempts to restore the death penalty were defeated in a historic 148-127 vote on June 30, 1987.

Bills to replace capital punishment with life imprisonment had been introduced in Parliament as early as 1914. Supporters argued the death penalty was barbaric, innocent people had been hanged, and produced studies showing it did not act as a deterrent.

The last execution in Canada — the double hanging of cop-killer Ronald Turpin, 29, and mob hitman Arthur Lucas, 54 — occurred at the Don Jail in Toronto at 12.02 a.m. on December 11,

1962. To that point, perhaps as many as 600 convicted criminals had been executed in the 95 years since Confederation.

It's not known how many met the hangman before Confederation. About 230 offences under British law were punishable by death in Canada in the century after France ceded its North American possession in 1763. These included stealing turnips, being disguised in a forest, buggery, burglary, arson, casting away a ship and exhibiting a false signal.

By Confederation, only murder, rape and treasonable offences remained as capital crimes.

The last public execution in Canada was the hanging of Patrick Whelan in Ottawa on February 11, 1869, for the assassination of Thomas D'Arcy McGee, a Father of Confederation.

Officials finally recognized that the public spectacle of a condemned wretch's final agony was not a deterrent to crime. Louts in festive crowds cheered and applauded those who stepped jauntily to their deaths and booed the fearful ones and those convicted of particularly heinous crimes. A hanging in York (Toronto) in 1828 drew 10,000 people, twice its population.

Two of Canada's most famous hangmen were John R. Radclive and Arthur English. Radclive who'd learned his trade hanging mutinous sailors from Royal Navy yardarms, came to Canada in the 1880s. He estimated he'd performed 200 executions — "I am 200 times a murderer," he said in an interview in 1912. English, who'd apprenticed under Britain's hangman, is believed to have performed 600 executions under the pseudonym Mr. Ellis, a name he took from an uncle, until retiring in 1936.

Their grisly part-time jobs destroyed both men. Both turned to drink. Both lost their families. "Now at night when I lie down, I start up with a roar as victim after victim comes up before me ... They taunt me and haunt me until I am nearly crazy with an unearthly fear," said Radclive, who downed a bottle of brandy after every execution. Ellis died in 1938 alone in a Montreal slum room of malnutrition and alcohol poisoning.

Missing persons
How do police check ID by dental records when they don't know the victim or the dentist?

The teeth of the deceased Jane or John Doe are charted by a dentist on a dental chart designed for use on the CPIC network (Canadian Police Information Computer) in Ottawa. Investigators hope to get a "hit" on the computer — names of missing persons whose dental records are compatible with the one submitted.

Authorities check out the records they are able to obtain as a result of names spewed out by the computer. If a possible match turns up, post mortem x-rays are compared with dental x-rays taken before a person went missing.

Citizens in police line-ups
When police have a suspect in a line-up, where do they get the other people to stand in the line-up?

"We usually go on to the street or among the general public and try to pick out people who will look very much like the suspect," said David Colwell, a detective in Metro Toronto police's downtown 52 Division.

"We tell them, 'We're trying to do a line-up and you look very much like the suspect. Would you mind coming in and helping us out in the line-up?'"

Why do police seek out look-alikes? "We have to give the suspect every benefit that we can," he said.

The volunteers are not paid. "And we can't force people, of course, to assist us," Colwell said. "But I've never known any instance where we haven't had lots of co-operation from the public."

Hotfoot
Is it illegal to drive barefoot in Canada?

No, just ill-advised. It's easier for your foot to slip off the brake pedal.

Good seed and bad
Is hemp as useful a plant as I've been hearing?

Hemp has been a major cash crop for thousands of years in other parts of the world. It's been cultivated for paper, canvas and other cloth, carpets, rope, twine and string, medicines, caulking, caged-bird feed, paints, varnishes, soaps, edible oil and other products.

And it grows like a weed.

Unfortunately, it is The Weed. "The botanical name is *cannabis sativa*," said Paul St. Denis of the federal Department of Justice. *Cannabis sativa* — hemp — is the marijuana plant. Marijuana and hashish are its best known products.

Hemp's cultivation has been prohibited in Canada since 1954 under an amendment to the then Opium and Narcotics Control Act because hemp was grown for marijuana and hashish, St. Denis said.

Marijuana first came under the act in 1923, added JoAnne Ford of the federal health department.

But hemp was never a big cash crop in this country (at least legally). Federal health department staff couldn't find mention of major industrial uses for hemp or any industries using hemp in Canada, going back to the early 1800s.

They did find an 1840 reference that complained that cultivation of hemp "was against the Will of The Lord."

"I guess people were smoking it then, using marijuana," Ford said.

Destroying booze, drugs
How are liquor and illegal drugs seized at the border destroyed?

When only a few bottles of liquor are involved at a customs or police outpost, the stuff may simply be poured down the sink.

For large caches of booze, the procedure varies according to the law under which it was seized, such as the Criminal Code of Canada or Customs Act, and practices of different agencies. But the method used has to comply with provincial environmental regulations.

Under the Customs Act and customs department policy, the alcohol is chemically altered and made harmless before disposal. Alcohol seized by the Royal Canadian Mounted Police may be disposed through recycling into other products.

For example, a Montreal firm under contract to the Mounties extracts and recycles the alcohol from liquor for industrial and commercial uses, such as in solvents and cleaners.

But disposal of narcotics comes under the jurisdiction of the federal minister of health, who is responsible for dangerous drugs under the Narcotic Control and Food and Drugs acts. Here's the routine, from Canada Customs, police agencies and Health Canada:

Because they are illegal drugs, Canada Customs turns any seizures of marijuana, heroin, cocaine, crack cocaine and such over to police.

After a case has been concluded — including appeal periods — police will make an application to the bureau of dangerous drugs at Health Canada to destroy drugs used as exhibits.

The bureau will authorize the destruction and prescribe the method to be used. Normally, they're burned in high-temperature commercial incinerators under government supervision.

Some drugs are chemically rendered inactive because their properties may cause a health or safety hazard if burned. Examples are methaqualone, a sleeping medication that's now illegal, and fentanyls, a narcotic.

The health minister may allow disposal of some drugs by returning them to police or customs for training purposes.

War and the traffic act

What is the only vehicle that can run a red light, cause an accident and not be held liable? A friend says it's a post office vehicle carrying a declaration of war. Right or wrong?

Fascinating conjecture. But why would anyone drop a declaration of war in the mail? Tim McGurrin at Canada Post in Ottawa checked with the corporation's lawyers anyway, and double-checked with the Department of National Defence.

Back came the replies, "Our legal department doesn't think in all probability we'd be given any special immunity as described by your questioner," McGurrin said.

Ditto for the defence department. Emergency vehicles, including military, "are expected to follow the rules of the road."

The only driver in Canada we could think of who could escape liability after causing an accident would be one with diplomatic status. "Foreign diplomats stationed in Canada are exempt from civil, criminal and administrative prosecution," confirmed Marthe St. Louis of the Department of Foreign Affairs in Ottawa.

But the infraction would be reported to foreign affairs and pressure could be applied on the diplomat or embassy to pay up, she said. Serious offences could lead to a diplomat's expulsion.

Canadian diplomats abroad are granted similar immunity. The government's policy is that our diplomats be "accountable and responsible."

For the record, police in Ottawa haven't encountered problems. "Diplomats usually are driven by chauffeurs, who don't have diplomatic status. They don't seem to put themselves in a position where they're driving," said Sgt. Michel Hebert of Ottawa-Carleton Regional Police.

Most of their chauffeurs are hired locally. Embassies are pretty good about paying whatever tickets and fines their drivers pick up.

Jobs in jails

In movies, you see convicts stamping out licence plates. Is this just dramatic licence or are plates actually produced in jails?
Inmates produce licence plates for the public, plus mattresses, foodstuff and other goods for use in provincial institutions. In Ontario, for example, about 1.5 million provincial licence plates a year — for cars, trucks, tractors, motorcycles, trailers, and so on — are turned out at Millbrook Correctional Centre in Millbrook, south of Peterborough.

The Ministry of Correctional Services has an industrial products division called Trilcor for Trillium Corrections, trillium being the provincial floral emblem. It supplies government institutions and non-profit agencies, but doesn't compete in the private sector.

"A lot of it is self-sufficiency," said John Hutton, manager of Trilcor, which has its headquarters in North Bay. "All the inmates' clothing is made through our shops. We have our own canning operation, which feeds our institutions — jams, juices."

Park benches, signs and recycling bins at provincial parks, and mattresses for provincial and federal institutions are among other products made in provincial correctional centers.

Inmates who produce goods, do laundry or clean the institutions are given an incentive allowance of $10 a week for canteen items.

The average stay in provincial institutions is 43 days, so much of Trilcor's efforts are geared to training inmates in jobs skills and in lifestyle skills to hold jobs, starting with getting to work on time.

Voodoo and the law
Is it illegal to practise voodoo in Canada?
Section 365 of the Criminal Code of Canada would apply to claims to "magic":

"Everyone who fraudulently (a) pretends to exercise or to use any kind of witchcraft, sorcery, enchantment or conjuration ... is guilty of an offence punishable on summary conviction."

But no court cases in Canada centered on the practice of voodoo as far as we could determine in checks with crown attorneys. Nor can we find any instances where practitioners snuck into courtrooms to sacrifice chickens on behalf of anyone accused of any crime, as they have in Florida.

Voodoo, or vodun, combining worship and the practice of magic, originated in Africa but is probably best known as the religious folk cult of Haiti. There it combines French colonial religious rituals of the 1700s with African religious and magical elements brought by slaves. The cult, with its legends of zombies, rising spirits and hexed voodoo dolls, is strongly opposed by the major churches.

Paid for duty at spectacles
How are police chosen for game duty at the SkyDome or Maple Leaf Gardens?
They volunteer for paid duty. That's a system where sports clubs, stores, concert promoters and so on hire off-duty police officers on a freelance basis to enhance their own security and normal policing.

The system is complicated, but basically officers who have rotated to the top of the pay-duty list get first crack on their days off when organizations call local division headquarters to engage them. The organization pays them at a time-and-a-half rate set by the police association. Commanders in each division decide what duties are acceptable.

Marriage among kinfolk
Is it legal to marry a cousin in Canada? An uncle, a nephew?
The answer to all three is yes, said Simon Fodden, a family law expert at York University's Osgoode Hall Law School. Here's how he explained the Canadian statutes:

Though most people don't know it, marriages between "cousins have always been legal. Relatively recently uncle-niece and aunt-nephew marriages have been made legal.

"In fact, there's a new law governing what are called prohibited degrees of consanguinity and affinity, which considerably liberalizes whom you may marry, the most significant change being that it is only degrees of consanguinity — that is, blood relationships — that are prohibited now in some respect.

"Degrees of affinity — people to whom you're related through marriage — your in-laws — are no longer prohibited in any respect."

This is what the Marriage (Prohibited Degrees) Act of 1990 states: "No person shall marry another person if they are related (a) lineally by consanguinity or adoption; (b) as brother and sister by consanguinity, whether by whole blood or by the half-blood; or (c) as brother and sister by adoption."

Related lineally means up and down the line, children, parents, grandparents, great grandparents. "The only addition to that is brother and sister," Fodden said.

Various religions and cultures may have stricter conventions governing marriages between blood relatives. For example, under Roman Catholic canon law, "Marriage is invalid between those related by consanguinity in all degrees of direct line ... In the collateral line (that means to the side) it is invalid up to the fourth degree inclusive."

The fourth degree is first cousins. The first degree is direct line — children, parents, grandparents. The second degree is brother and sister, including half-siblings and adopted. The third is uncle-niece, aunt-nephew.

In certain grave cases — say, where it is a tradition in certain societies — dispensation can be given by the bishop to allow first cousins to wed within the church, but it is not encouraged, said Suzanne Scorsone, speaking for the Chancellor of Spiritual Affairs in the Archdiocese of Toronto.

Scorsone, an anthropologist by training, could conceive of no situation where a third-degree marriage could be celebrated in the diocese.

Suicide reports

Since coming to Canada from Britain, we've never read a news report of a suicide. Are there laws banning the publication of such reports?

There's no law against reporting suicides. But as a general rule Canadian newspapers feel it is an unnecessary intrusion into a family's grief to publicize the cause of a death as suicide.

There are exceptions to this rule, such as when the suicide is that of a prominent public individual or when there is an overriding public interest in knowing the cause of death.

5

WHO'S WHAT IN CANADA

One in 510 Canadians is a lawyer
Is it true that one in every 600 people in the United States is a lawyer, compared to one in 10,000 in Japan?
The figures, including those for Canada, are more astonishing than that if they are correct.

Here are statistics provided by the U.S. and Japanese embassies in Ottawa and by Statistics Canada:

The 1991 Canadian census shows a population of 27,296,859. Of these, 53,570 people listed their occupation as lawyers and notaries, 165,995 were engineers, and 66,020 were medical doctors.

The U.S. population in 1991 was approximately 253,000,000. Of these, 744,000 people were lawyers, 1,846,000 were engineers, and 575,000 were medical doctors.

Japanese figures show a 1990 population of 124,130,000. The Japanese Federation of Bar Associations' current count is 14,926 lawyers. (That would include everyone we term barristers and solicitors, the embassy says). The 1990 estimate of engineers was 2,250,800, and medical doctors numbered 211,797.

(In all the above figures, engineer includes chemical, civil, electrical, industrial, agricultural engineers, and so on; doctor includes chiropractors, but not dentists or veterinarians; the heading lawyer doesn't include judges).

Crunch those figures into a calculator and this is what comes out:

In Canada, one in every 510 people is a lawyer; one in every 164 is an engineer and one in every 414 is a doctor.

In the United States, there is one lawyer for every 340 people, one engineer for every 137 and one doctor for every 440.

In Japan, there's one engineer for every 55 people, one medical doctor for every 586 and one lawyer for every 8,316 people (though it's been suggested the ratio is incorrect, arguing the Japanese count and definition of lawyers differ from the West's).

Draw your own conclusions.

Charting the jobless
How does Statistics Canada know how many people are unemployed?

Canada was in a recession when we looked into this. Statistics Canada had just reported the national unemployment rate was 11.1 per cent.

It had measured the work force at 14,044,000 people, seasonally adjusted, and found 12,487,000 were employed and 1,559,000 were unemployed. Of those employed, 10,298,000 worked full-time and 2,189,000 part-time.

To obtain such figures and much more, StatsCan's labour force survey covers about 58,000 households each month involving about 103,000 people across the ten provinces. The two territories aren't included because of small populations and enormous areas.

The survey, usually conducted during the week that includes the 15th day of the month, is designed to represent everybody within Canada 15 years and older outside Indian reserves, the military or living in institutions.

The first interviews are done in the home but subsequently may be taken by telephone. A household remains in the sample for about six months.

A survey that size is considered accurate to within 0.3 percentage points, plus or minus. That's ten times sharper than a political survey of 1,000 people, with a margin of error of 3 per cent either way, 19 out of 20 times.

The term "seasonally adjusted" means that seasonal, cyclical and irregular factors have been eliminated. It's a complicated computer program, using historical data.

Top of the pay scale
What are the best-paid occupations in Canada? Salary is an important consideration as I make career choices.

Average wages are very different for men and for women, according to the Statistics Canada list of top average incomes for full-time workers from the 1991 census.

For example, judges and magistrates lead the list of highest paying occupations in Canada with an annual average salary of $102,646.

Physicians and surgeons were number two, averaging $102,370 after expenses but before taxes. But male physicians and surgeons were at the top of the pay list, earning almost $2,000 more than male judges. Male doctors averaged $111,261, compared to the $73,071 earned by female colleagues.

Male judges and magistrates earned $109,313. Women judges averaged $79,204, which is $6,000 more than women doctors got.

A StatsCan study, however, showed women were earning more than their spouses in a quarter of dual-income families in 1993, and women were the breadwinners in 20 per cent of families where only one of the spouses was working, up from 2 per cent in 1967.

The main reason was the number of husbands who lost manufacturing and managerial jobs during the deep recession in the early '90s, while the wives were in service-sector jobs that weathered the recession. Men, usually older than their spouses, were also retiring earlier.

The average pay in the census data is based on average annual earnings across Canada for men and for women working full-time.

Following is the pay for men and, in brackets, for women in the rest of the ten highest-paying occupations in descending order of average combined salaries: dentists $99,280 ($67,997); lawyers and notaries $86,108 ($50,012); general managers, senior officials $74,425 ($40,633); managers, administrators in mines, oil wells, etc. $73,281 ($39,151); airline pilots, navigators, etc. $66,087 ($31,026); osteopaths and chiropractors $68,404 ($45,368); engineering, natural sciences $66,668 ($41,800) and university teachers $65,671 ($49,000).

While professional Canadian athletes were in the top ten — making an average of $67,839 in 1990 — their very small numbers rendered their income statistics unreliable, StatsCan said.

As a comparison, here are average combined salaries in other occupations: sales agents and traders securities (including stock-brokers) $51,308; high school teachers $44,970; elementary school teachers $39,409; construction electricians $37,399; plumbers and pipefitters $36,229, and construction laborers $30,323.

Bottom of the pay scale
The only jobs open seem to be minimum wage. What are the lowest-paying jobs? How do salaries in day care compare?
Women in child-care occupations were near the bottom of the list of lowest-paying occupations in Canada, Statistics Canada figures show.

Lowest paid workers of all were women in crop farming, according to an incomes survey of one-fifth of the population in the 1991 census.

In fact, average pay in all categories for full-time work was much lower for women than for men. For example, the average annual income across Canada in child care was $13,518. The 1,440 men counted full time in this category earned an average of $20,987, compared to the $13,252 averaged by the 40,365 women counted.

Food and beverage servers averaged about $14,100 a year, the second lowest on the list. There were 13,845 men and 48,505 women counted in this category. Women earned an average of $13,037, while men averaged $17,822.

The average income for women and, in brackets, men from the ten lowest-paying occupations, and starting with the lowest female-male combined average income: child care $13,252 ($20,987); housekeepers, servants, etc. $14,053 ($19,210); service station attendants $13,359 ($16,135); lodging cleaners $15,178 ($19,238); bartenders $13,952 ($18,558); crop farm workers $12,421 ($19,814); other farming, horticultural $12,174 ($19,537); sewing machine operators, textile, etc. $15,933 ($22,991); livestock farm workers $11,788 ($19,279).

Trappers and hat-makers would have been listed among the ten lowest-paying occupations except so few of them are left StatsCan considered their income statistics unreliable.

High income families
How rare is an income of $250,000 a year or more?

One per cent of Canadian families had an average income of $295,000 a year, according to a study of high income families based on the 1991 census. That's about 73,600 households.

High income was defined as earnings of $185,000 or more. About 5,150 families — 7 per cent of the 1 per cent — earned more than $500,000. And 5 per cent had an income between $400,000 and $500,000.

The income came from various sources, but mainly from wages and an average $68,000 from investments.

Abdul Rashid, responsible for income data in the census, said high income isn't necessarily a synonym for rich or wealthy. "A young family with high income may not have yet accumulated large assets, while an elderly couple without a large current income may have substantial wealth holdings," the study said.

Meanwhile, the overall average income for families at the time of the study stood at $51,300.

At the bottom of the income scale, about 5 per cent of families reported incomes of less than $6,000.

French in Canada
How many people speak French in Canada, and by province?
Statistics Canada measured this in various ways during the 1991 census: language most often spoken at home, knowledge of the official languages, and mother tongue, which refers to the first language learned in childhood and still understood.

Out of a total Canadian population of 26,994,040, the '91 census shows 6,502,865 people listed French as their mother tongue.

By province: Newfoundland, 2,770 people; Prince Edward Island, 5,590; Nova Scotia, 36,635; New Brunswick, 241,565; Quebec, 5,556,105; Ontario, 485,395; Manitoba, 49,130; Saskatchewan, 20,885; Alberta, 53,715, and British Columbia 48,835. The number in the Yukon Territory was 865 people and in the Northwest Territories, 1,375.

During the 1995 Quebec Referendum campaign, Prime Minister Jean Chretien noted that across Canada about 300,000 non-francophone students were in French immersion courses.

Group of Ten
Who were the members of the Group of Seven?
In all, ten artists were members of the Toronto-based group who travelled the Canadian wilderness, capturing the "spirit of the land" in expressive, individualistic ways far different from the popular style of their day.

An outline of the painters was provided by the McMichael Canadian Art Collection in Kleinburg, Ont., which has more than 1,000 of their works in its collection.

The founding seven were Franklin Carmichael, Lawren Harris, A.Y. Jackson, Franz Johnston, Arthur Lismer, J.E.H. MacDonald and F.H. Varley. They worked together before World War I, but did not hold their first major exhibition as the Group of Seven until May 1920.

Johnston left after that exhibition. A.J. Casson joined in 1926, and Edwin Holgate and Lionel LeMoine FitzGerald became part of the group before it disbanded in the early 1930s.

Tom Thomson shared the ideals that shaped the group's visions and joined them on sketching trips, but died on a canoe trek in 1917 before the group officially came into existence.

Lawren Harris wrote in *The Story of the Group of Seven*, "On all our camping and sketching trips, we learned to explore each region for those particular areas where form and character and spirit reached its summation — the spirit of the land."

Birth on the water
If a baby is born over international waters, what nationality would the infant be?

Most countries give citizenship either by "birth on the soil" (*jus soli*) or "birth by blood line" (*jus sanguinis*).

In Canada, both concepts apply, said Norman Sabourin, a director in the citizenship registration branch of the Department of Citizenship and Immigration.

And the principles extend over international waters. If one of the parents is Canadian, the baby is considered a Canadian citizen under Canadian law, even if born on a foreign carrier.

A baby born on a Canadian-registered carrier is considered Canadian-born under Canadian law, even if both parents are foreigners. The parents can obtain a certificate of citizenship for the child if they wish.

Whether the infant is allowed dual citizenship (or tri-citizenship when the parents are of different foreign nationalities) is up to the other country involved. Canada recognizes dual citizenship.

Allegiance and citizenship
How many Canadians have dual citizenship?

Almost 400,000, according to Statistics Canada. Data from the 1991 census show 70,055 Canadians by birth and 325,230 naturalized Canadians listed "other citizenship" as well. That's about 1.5 per cent of the 25,465,640 men, women and children who are Canadian citizens, native born or naturalized.

Canada's population in 1991 totalled more than 27 million people, about 22.5 million of whom were born in Canada. The immigrant population numbered about 4.4 million, and 225,000 people were non-permanent residents.

More and more countries — including Canada since 1977 — allow native-born citizens to take out citizenship in countries of their parents' birth and do not require immigrants, on naturalization, to renounce citizenship in another country. "Canada recognizes that the authority of who is or who isn't a citizen of another country, is the privilege of the other country," said Sabourin.

But a parliamentary committee in 1994 recommended restricting or abolishing dual citizenship. It questioned how it's possible to swear loyalty and allegiance to more than one country.

Eligibility varies among countries where dual citizenship is permitted. Some have strict requirements, such as residency, and still others allow multi-citizenship when parents were born in different countries. Other countries like China, India, Poland and South Africa don't allow dual citizenship.

Neither did Canada prior to 1977, before current legislation came into force, Sabourin said. "You would lose Canadian citizenship if you voluntarily obtained citizenship of another country."

The original Canada Citizenship Act was passed in 1947, the first statute to define Canadians. Until 1947, Canadians — both native born and naturalized — were, under naturalization acts, British subjects.

The People
When and why did Eskimos become Inuit?
They've always called themselves Inuit — it just means "the people" in their language — but missionaries called them Eskimos. (They misunderstood and mispronounced a word used by native people to the south.)

Inuit has been the preferred word since the northerners rallied political clout in the early 1970s. The Inuit Tapirisat, their national organization, says a few still call themselves Eskimos but most consider that name a slur.

The singular is Inuk. The language is Inuktituk. And don't confuse Inuit with Innu, an unrelated native band in Labrador.

And don't call them *the* Inuit

Canadians at worship
How many Canadians go to church every Sunday?

More than 6.2 million Canadians attended worship services at least once a week at their church, temple, synagogue or hall.

The estimate is taken from a 1992 general social survey provided by Statistics Canada. It was based on interviews with 21,294 Canadians over 15 years of age on frequency of attendance at a place of worship.

A total of 4,890, or 23 per cent, indicated they went to worship at least once a week. No doubt many were accompanied by children 15 and younger. Twenty-three per cent of Canada's 27 million population translates into 6,210,000 people who worship at least once a week.

But as many Canadians seem to have left the fold. About 23 per cent of those who listed affiliation with formal religions told the StatsCan survey they never attend worship services at all.

About 11 per cent of those surveyed said they attended worship at least once a month, 20 per cent several times a year and 7 per cent at least once a year. About 13 per cent said they had no religious affiliation.

Attendance at worship continues to decline in Canada. In 1990, 24 per cent of adults attended weekly, StatsCan says. In 1985, it was 27 per cent.

Identical quints
Were the Dionne quintuplets identical or fraternal twins?

Annette, Cecile, Emilie, Marie and Yvonne Dionne may be described as identical, from the same genetic material. Fraternal twins come from two different eggs fertilized at the same time; identical twins from a single egg that has divided.

A biological study at the University of Toronto established that the quints — born prematurely near Callander, Ont., on May 28, 1934 — originated from a single cell mass and arose through repeated twinnings. Six embryos were produced, but one aborted early in the pregnancy.

Prior to the Dionnes, not one member of any known previous set of quintuplets lived more than a few days. Emilie died in 1954 and Marie in 1970.

Hudson Bay castaways

Whatever happened to Henry Hudson? Was he eaten by his crew?

The English navigator (1565-1611) who searched for Arctic routes to Asia was seized by mutineers after wintering in James Bay and set adrift in an open boat with his son, John, and seven loyal crewmen. The castaways were never seen again.

Suicide rates

What is Canada's suicide rate?

It runs about 13 deaths per 100,000 people. That is a bit worse than the U.S. rate but a lot better than at least 15 other countries, e.g. Hungary (40), Sri Lanka (38) or Finland (27). The World Health Organization does not rank nations by suicide rates.

Canadian males kill themselves four times as often as females. Among both sexes, the age groups especially prone to suicide are 20-25 and over 65.

6

TYPICAL CANADIAN HEROES

Prodigal fathers

Who are the Fathers of Confederation and what were their backgrounds? When you go to look them up, most are just names on a list. Only the most prominent have bios.

The Fathers of Confederation are the archetypical Canadian heroes. Many Canadians can name only one for sure — but what of the spelling — Macdonald? MacDonald? McDonald?

Most are anonymous. Not even the federal government they designed recognizes them. No act of Parliament or order-in-council defines Fathers of Confederation. No official proclamation mentions them. Their names are not writ in stone on hallowed ground. They're not even writ on official bond paper. Requests for an official biographical list turned up zero at the Library of Parliament, the National Archives and the House of Commons' information office. An official list doesn't exist.

One of the reasons for this lack of popular recognition is that there are too many of them — 36, or more. The exact number depends on how Fathers of Confederation are defined. Another is they're dead.

But historians aren't unanimous on whom exactly belongs in the pantheon. Definitions sometimes include representatives of the Red River Colony who created Manitoba in 1870; Louis Riel, who fomented rebellion to create a better nation for Métis and Indians; those who brought Newfoundland into Canada in 1949, particularly Joey Smallwood.

Others mentioned are the politicians who brought British Columbia into the federation in 1871 or the mostly Ontario emigres who brought in Saskatchewan and Alberta in 1905.

But it's generally accepted that the basic list numbers 36, the politicians from the united Canadas — Quebec and Ontario now — and the Maritimes who attended at least one of the three conferences that led to Confederation in 1867.

Here, in alphabetical order, is the list of the original 36 political leaders who attended any of the three Confederation conferences and thus became, under the generally accepted definition, Fathers of Confederation:

Sir Adams George Archibald (1814-1892), lawyer, born at Truro, represented Nova Scotia as opposition leader. He was a strong supporter of Confederation at the Charlottetown Conference on Maritimes union and the Quebec and London conferences on the wider union.

George Brown (1818-1880), born in Scotland, founder of *The Globe* (now *The Globe and Mail*) newspaper in Toronto, and a reform-minded political leader. He was a delegate from the Legislative Assembly of the Province of Canada at Charlottetown and Quebec. He was slain 13 years after Confederation by a fired employee at his newspaper.

Sir Alexander Campbell (1822-1892), a lawyer, born in England. He was a delegate for the united Canadas at the Charlottetown and Quebec conferences.

Sir Frederick Bowker T. Carter (1819-1900), a lawyer, born in St. John's, and head of Newfoundland's delegation to Quebec as speaker of the house. As Newfoundland premier, he was defeated on the Confederation issue in 1869.

Sir George-Étienne Cartier (1814-1873), a lawyer, born in St. Antoine, and political leader from Lower Canada who believed French Canada's distinctiveness could best be protected in a federation. He was a pivotal figure for Confederation at all three conferences.

Edward Barron Chandler (1800-1880), lawyer, born in Amherst, N.S. He was at Charlottetown and Quebec as a member of the New Brunswick executive council. He favored Confederation but was wary of strong powers for the central government.

Jean-Charles Chapais (1811-1885), merchant, born in Riviere-Ouelle, attended Quebec conference as member of the Canadian cabinet.

James Cockburn (1819-1883), lawyer, born in England, delegate at Quebec as solicitor-general in the Canadian cabinet. He later became the first speaker of the new federal Parliament.

George H. Coles (1810-1875), businessman, born in Prince Edward Island, which he represented at Charlottetown and Quebec as reform leader. He and his reform colleagues opposed strong powers for the central government and delayed the island's entry into Confederation.

Robert Barry Dickey (1811-1903), lawyer, born in Amherst, appointed to the Nova Scotia legislative council and chosen as a conservative delegate to Charlottetown and to Quebec. He favored the principle of Confederation but also worried too much power was being given to the central government.

Charles Fisher (1808-1880), born in Fredericton, was a reform premier and champion of responsible government in New Brunswick. He attended the Quebec Conference and, as New Brunswick's attorney-general, helped frame the British North America Act at the London Conference.

Sir Alexander Tilloch Galt (1817-1893), businessman-administrator, born in England. In political life, from Quebec in the united Canadas, he was an early advocate of Confederation and a key figure at all three conferences, particularly in making Confederation financially workable.

John Hamilton Gray (1811-1887), one of two Fathers of Confederation by that name, was born in Prince Edward Island, had a military career before entering politics. He was host premier at Charlottetown and a delegate at Quebec, favoring union though many islanders did not.

John Hamilton Gray (1814-1889), this one a lawyer and born in Bermuda, a delegate from the New Brunswick legislature at Charlottetown and Quebec. He wrote a history of events there. He helped define the legislative powers of the federal and provincial parliaments.

Thomas Heath Haviland (1822-1895), a lawyer, born in Charlottetown, was a representative on the island's expanded delegation to Quebec. He favored union and was one of three commissioners who worked out terms for P.E.I.'s entry in 1873.

William Alexander Henry (1816-1888), a lawyer, born in Halifax. As Nova Scotia's attorney-general he was at Charlottetown, Quebec and London. He advocated the elected government be able to create new senators to override opposition in the appointed Senate (the clause was used in 1990 to ram the goods and services tax through the Senate).

William Pearce Howland (1811-1907), Toronto businessman, born in New York, and reform advocate in the united Canadas assembly. He was finance minister and a substitute delegate at London for Oliver Mowat. He urged senators be appointed for a fixed term by the provinces.

John Mercer Johnson (1818-1868), a lawyer, born in England. He held a number of portfolios in the New Brunswick government and was chosen a delegate at all three conferences. At Quebec, he denounced the strong powers given to the federal government.

Sir Hector-Louis Langevin (1826-1906), a lawyer, born in Quebec City, also believed that the culture of the continent's French-speaking people could best be protected within a Canadian confederacy, and was among the united Canadas delegates at all three conferences.

Andrew Archibald Macdonald (1829-1912) born in P.E.I., a merchant and ship owner who was a delegate from the island's legislative council at Charlottetown and Quebec. He spoke out against the federal plan and urged increased Senate representation from the Maritimes.

Sir John A. (Alexander) Macdonald (1815-1891), lawyer, born in Scotland and raised in Kingston, a pivotal figure in Confederation as premier of the Canadas. He was able to focus divergent views and lead deliberations toward forging a consensus on Confederation, at Charlottetown, Quebec and as chairman of the London Conference. He became Canada's first Prime Minister.

Jonathan McCully (1809-1877), teacher, lawyer, editor, born in Nova Scotia, and an opposition member of the legislative council chosen as a delegate to the talks at Charlottetown, Quebec and London. He was one of the most enthusiastic advocates of Confederation.

William McDougall (1822-1905), lawyer, born near Toronto, delegate for the united Canadas at Charlottetown, Quebec and London. After Confederation, he arranged along with Cartier for the transfer of Hudson's Bay Co. lands to Canada.

Thomas D'Arcy McGee (1825-1868), journalist, born in Ireland and a supporter of the British connection in the Canadas. He was at Charlottetown and Quebec and had spoken passionately of his vision of a great new nation. He was assassinated in 1868, allegedly by a Fenian extremist.

Peter Mitchell (1824-1899), a lawyer and businessman, born in Newcastle, N.B., he represented New Brunswick at the Quebec and London conferences. He strongly supported Confederation, though it was rejected by New Brunswick electors in 1865, and helped reverse that tide in an election a year later.

Sir Oliver Mowat (1820-1903), a lawyer, born in Kingston, served at the Quebec Conference as a cabinet minister from the united Canadas and framed the resolution on the legislative powers of provincial governments. He served as Ontario premier from 1872-96.

Edward Palmer (1809-1889), lawyer, born in Charlottetown. He attended the Charlottetown and Quebec Conferences, opposing Confederation, calling himself the "malcontent" of the Quebec talks. Later, he favored the terms that brought P.E.I. into the fold in 1873.

William Henry Pope (1825-1879), lawyer, born in Prince Edward Island, supported the idea of union at Charlottetown and Quebec conferences, going against the flow of other representatives from the island. He steadfastly continued his campaign until success in 1873.

John William Ritchie (1808-1890), lawyer, born in Annapolis, N.S., supported Confederation for its commercial and economic advantages. His work as a cabinet minister on provinces' commercial committees led to his appointment to the London Conference on the N.S. delegation.

Sir Ambrose Shea (1815-1905), businessman, born in St. John's, and delegate to the Quebec Conference as Newfoundland's opposition leader in the assembly. He was a staunch supporter of union as a means of boosting the island's economy, but the idea was so bitterly opposed at home that he was forced to abandon his dream.

William Henry Steeves (1814-1873), businessman, born in Hillsborough, N.B., backed freer trade and intercolonial railway for British North America. His work led to his appointment with other N.B. politicians to Charlottetown and Quebec as a member of the legislative council.

Sir Étienne-Paschal Taché (1795-1865), medical doctor, born at St. Thomas de Montmagny, had left politics because of ill health when he was called out of retirement to bring leadership to a chaotic political situation. He presided at Quebec as first minister of the host province and defended the resolutions that shaped Confederation.

Sir Samuel Leonard Tilley (1818-1896), businessman, born at Gagetown, N.B. He quit school at 13 but became a success in business and politics. As New Brunswick premier, he worked for union at the talks in Charlottetown and Quebec despite sentiment against it at home. It cost him an electoral defeat in 1865. He was returned a year later and pushed for the final conference in London.

Sir Charles Tupper (1821-1915), medical doctor, born in Amherst, N.S. He was an advocate of Maritime Union but then worked for the wider union as Nova Scotia's chief delegate at all three conferences. He worked vigorously within the province to keep the dream alive against fierce opposition. He became the sixth prime minister.

Edward Whelan (1824-1867), journalist, born in Ireland and brought to Prince Edward Island as a boy. He was a strong supporter of union despite its unpopularity on the island. It cost him his seat in 1867. He'd attended the Quebec conference as a P.E.I cabinet minister.

Robert Duncan Wilmot (1809-1891), businessman, born in New Brunswick, a reform politician favoring a union that would do away with provincial legislatures. He originally opposed the terms because he felt provinces were left with too much authority. He was among New Brunswick ministers at the London Conference, where the British North America Act was drafted.

So there they are: 36 middle-class white men in 19th-century suits — some distinguished, some ordinary.

None is credited with the god-like wisdom and foresight usually granted founders of other countries by their succeeding generations, but all deserve a mention, at least, on that one day in the year that marks the day Confederation came to pass in 1867. But even on July 1, does anybody recall them?

Canucks beat Edison to light bulb
Is it true that Thomas Edison had the help of two Canadian scientists in inventing the electric light bulb?

The invention of the incandescent electric light is credited to American genius Thomas Alva Edison in 1879 — but two Canadians beat him to it.

They produced light in a bulb in Toronto by heating a carbon filament using its resistance to electricity, six years before Edison announced the discovery.

Their invention was, in at least one respect, more advanced than Edison's, using nitrogen in the bulb as is done today.

But Edison bought the rights to their patent while he was conducting his own experiments, trying to perfect a bulb to light the world.

The names of the two Canadians — Henry Woodward, a medical student at the University of Toronto, and Matthew Evans, a Toronto hotel keeper — were lost to history because investors backed off from the enormous costs of exploiting their invention.

Woodward and Evans were neighbors who frequently got together to experiment with Woodward's large battery and an induction coil. At dusk on a late winter day in 1873, they noticed the light from the spark at the contact post.

According to a 1990 report in the *Electrical News*, Evans drew out his watch and exclaimed: "Look at the light from the spark! Why you can even see the time!"

"My!" said Woodward, "if one could only confine that in a globe of some sort, what an invention we would have! It would revolutionize the world!"

The first incandescent lamp was constructed at Morrison's Brass Foundry on Adelaide St. W. in Toronto. Documents described it as "consisting of a water gauge glass with a piece of carbon filed by hand and drilled at each end for the electrodes and hermetically sealed at both ends."

After exhausting the air in it, Woodward filled the bulb with nitrogen. The Canadians' patent suggests that, after the air is extracted, the bulb be "filled with rarefied gas that will not unite chemically with the carbon when hot."

In his patent, Edison would later call for a nearly perfect vacuum "to prevent oxidation and injury to the conductor by the atmosphere."

After Edison's discovery, a Professor Thomas proclaimed that if

Woodward had not filled the bulb with nitrogen after exhausting the air, "He would have had the honor of being the inventor of the incandescent light as used for commercial purposes."

But in fact, the Woodward and Evans lamp was years ahead of Edison's in this. Bulbs today of 40 watts or more contain a mixture of gases, usually argon and nitrogen for longer life and to prevent arcing inside the bulb.

The Woodward and Evans invention worked in the same way lamps work today, connected in a circuit similar to one Edison devised. In the mid-1870s, six of their lamps were connected in a series to demonstrate their incandescence to promoters who'd come together to finance the discovery's commercial applications.

But by this time, financiers balked at putting more money into the development of the invention. In disgust, Woodward sailed to England and abandoned his efforts. Evans, who'd already spent $20,000 of his own money in perfecting the incandescent light, didn't have the resources to carry on alone.

Edison, already a wealthy and famous inventor, had the resources at his discovery factory in Menlo Park, N.J., where he'd invented the phonograph. A syndicate of industrialists advanced him $50,000 and formed Edison Electric Light Co. after he announced in September 1878, that he planned to invent a safe and inexpensive electric light to replace gaslight.

Many of the world's greatest inventions evolved from previous pioneering work. So it was with the incandescent electric light bulb. Woodward and Evans didn't get the credit for inventing it. They never even got credit for helping to light the way for the discovery.

Tabs for chairs
Is it true that you can exchange aluminum can pull-tabs for wheelchairs? How? Why not use the whole can?

This is one of those subjects that fall under the heading Strange, but True. The swap used to be a hoax, a tabs-for-wheelchairs joke. Then two guys who'd been duped came along in the 1980s and gave it a happy ending. The story begins with two nice guys left holding the bag on a useless mountain of pull-tab rings.

But let's start with the ending: Ray Pearse and Jack Baumber estimate they've sold maybe 500 million of pull-tabs tabs from beer and pop cans as scrap aluminum since 1989 and at last count raised enough money for 93 wheelchairs.

They did it in their spare time. Pearse, of Fergus, Ont., was chief steward at the Legion Branch 229 in nearby Elora until he retired. Baumber, of Elora, worked with him as the Legion branch's caretaker.

The rings — pull-tabs and the new push-tabs — come from collectors in households, schools, small factories, big plants, taverns, stores, community drives and some Legionhalls in just about every community in Ontario, with bags and bushels coming in from the rest of Canada.

Pearse and Baumber early on talked big business into pitching in. Now, fleets of truck drivers pick up piles of tabs across Ontario and drop them off at the loading dock at the W.C. Wood Co. Ltd. in Guelph, one of NorthAmerica's biggest appliance manufacturers.

From there, the two men load the tabs on to Baumber's pickup truck and head for the Alcan Aluminum recycling smelter in Guelph. They're paid dealers' prices, 40-odd cents a pound and up (80 cents a kilo plus), twice as much as they'd been getting from scrap yards.

They needed all the help they could get. They've moved a mountain — 500 million rings, after all — that's eked out more than $100,000 for the chairs. The response to the immense undertaking surprised even them. "We figured it would take three or four years to get one wheelchair," Baumber said.

"Let me put it this way," Pearse said. "There's 1,000 pop-can tabs in a pound. It takes approximately two tons to buy a wheelchair. So you're looking at four million tabs. Now that's just a straight wheelchair."

An ordinary wheelchair costs about $1,000. A motorized, prescription wheelchair runs from about $2,500 up.

Through volunteer drivers and direct deliveries from collectors, as many as four million tab rings (more than 1,800 kilograms, or 4,000 pounds) have arrived in one week, Pearse said.

They were lucky to eke out 227 kilograms (about 500 pounds) on a good week when they approached Alcan for help a year after launching their campaign.

"Normally, we don't accept that small a quantity," said Peter Della Via, general manager of Alcan's recycling alloys plant in Guelph. "We're a large smeltering facility and we usually buy in 20,000- or 30,000-pound lots."

But he made an exception for Pearse and Baumber. "What the heck, it's a decent cause, so we take it in." Della Via was a bit reluctant to talk about what might be construed as the aluminum giant's heart of gold. The thought of people lining up outside the gates with pockets or pails full of the tabs is enough to give him nightmares. He'd have to turn them away.

Ontario's haulers also took up the cause. Owen Agla, fleet warehouse manager at W.C. Wood, said they got involved when he heard from truck-driving Legionnaires that Pearse and Baumber had no way of getting the tabs picked up.

Pearse and Baumber's biggest problem is trying to figure out how to get loads of tabs from other parts of Canada. They plan to persuade interprovincial haulers to collect those tab motherlodes.

In the late 1970s and into the 1980s, the pull-tab for wheelchairs scheme was a popular hoax, set up by practical jokers to waste a community's time. The idea was to have volunteers work an entire day collecting, say, 1,000 tabs. The seven or eight hours' work would be worth only pennies if they could find a scrap dealer to take them. Volunteers driving around town picking up a trunk full from the collectors would spend more on gasoline than the stuff was worth.

And then they were left holding the bag. Nobody gave away wheelchairs for pull-tabs. But people continued to collect the tabs, believing in a cause that defied economic logic and common sense.

Over the years, a supply built up in basements, garages, attics, stores and factories as good-hearted people awaited ... well, awaited Pearse and Baumber.

Lesser men would have tossed the damned things out. Pearse and Baumber were undaunted. "We thought the idea of getting a wheelchair for tabs was not a bad idea," Pearse said.

Not bad, indeed.

Mrs. O'Malley's flag

Does Canada have a Betsy Ross, a seamstress who sewed the first flag? Or was it done by committee?

Canada has Joan O'Malley. She sewed the first Maple Leaf flag ever flown. It was one of four prototypes made during a stormy night in December 1964, by Mrs. O'Malley, a 20-year-old newlywed.

Prime Minister Lester Pearson had asked to have the nation's proposed flag raised at his Harrington Lake retreat the following morning. He wanted to see how it would look flying over Canadian countryside.

But only drawings by its designer, George Stanley, were available.

MP John Matheson, Pearson's flag expert, and Patrick Reid of the Canadian Government Exhibitions Commission drove over to the old Department of Trade and Commerce offices in Ottawa at 4:30, looking for bunting to make up the flag.

Ken Donovan, the assistant purchasing chief for the department, went on a shopping expedition and found 30 yards of white bunting at a camping equipment store in Hull just before closing. Graphic artist Jean Desrosiers silkscreened the flag designs, the red 11-point maple leaf and red bunting for the borders.

But officials didn't have anybody to put it together. Seamstress and tailor shops had shut early because of the storm. By 9:30 p.m. they were still looking.

Matheson and Reid turned to Donovan. Did he know anyone who sewed well enough to make the flag? Donovan remembered his daughter had a little Singer sewing machine to make her own dresses. "Well, I could phone my daughter. Maybe she'd be interested."

He reached her at home by telephone. "Busy?" he asked. O'Malley went down to her basement to get the sewing machine. Her husband, Brian, drove her over to Kaladar Ave. There, she went to work.

After hectic hours of sewing heavy bunting on the little machine while nervous officials fretted and worried around her, Mrs. O'Malley finished the task. "Thank God that's over. I'm tired," she told them.

They swore her to secrecy and sent her home.

Three of the flags she'd sewn featured the single maple leaf and one, Stanley's alternate design, had three maple leafs on a single stem, as depicted on Canada's Coat of Arms. Stanley preferred the single leaf for its simplicity.

Donovan dropped off his daughter's work at the prime minister's residence, 24 Sussex Drive in the middle of the night. The next morning, after the storm, the Maple Leaf flag flew for the first time, raised unofficially and in great secrecy at Harrington Lake. Only a deeply moved Pearson and a handful of others witnessed the event.

On the following February, Mrs. O'Malley flag became the first Maple Leaf flag ever raised over the Peace Tower on Parliament Hill.

Professional seamstress Betsy Ross, who sewed the first Stars and Stripes flag for the U.S. in her shop in 1777, earned £14 pounds for the job. She became a national heroine.

In Canada, Mrs. O'Malley is a footnote to history, but her flags were a better bargain. She wasn't paid a cent and wouldn't have accepted if payment had been offered, and it was not. "I don't think you could be paid for something like that. I would never, ever take payment for doing something for my country," she said.

The Maple Leaf flag first raised over Parliament was later presented to the federal exhibition commission for safekeeping. Eventually, it was supposed to go to the Museum of Civilization in Hull. Another was given to Queen's University. The whereabouts of the third single-leaf prototype and the three-leaf alternate are unknown.

As for the old Singer, the last time we talked Mrs. O'Malley was still sewing with it.

Radio's Canadian inventor
Are there any monuments to scientist Reginald Aubrey Fessenden anywhere in Canada?

Yes, your AM radio. This almost forgotten Canadian physicist not only invented it but was the world's first broadcaster, among a number of other firsts.

Almost a year before Guglielmo Marconi gained immortality by receiving the Morse letter "S" in a trans-Atlantic wireless transmission to St. John's, Nfld. in 1901, Fessenden's voice was on the airwaves from a microphone hooked up to a Morse transmitter he'd altered: "One, two, three, four. Is it snowing where you are, Mr. Thiessen? If so telegraph back and let me know."

Thiessen was 80 kilometres away in Arlington, Va., where Fessenden had set up a receiver he'd developed.

A few moments later, the telegraph began dotting and dashing at Fessenden's U.S. Weather Service lab on Cobb Island on the Potomac River. Yes, it was snowing in Arlington.

For the first time in history, the human voice had been transmitted by electromagnetic waves, by radio.

Five years later, precisely at 9 p.m. on December 24, 1906, astounded wireless operators on ships off the east coast heard Fessenden's voice introducing a Christmas program, an Ediphone recording of Handel's "Largo," and then Fessenden on the violin playing "O, Holy Night," and singing the last verse.

That was the world's first radio program. Awed listeners confirmed he'd invented a way to transmit the human voice over long distances and without wires.

Fessenden's inventions for voice transmission were the first to successfully modulate the amplitude of radio waves into the shape of sound waves — in effect, AM (amplitude modulation) radio.

He was born in 1866 near Sherbrooke, Que., and educated at

Trinity College School in Port Hope, Ont., and Bishop's University in Quebec. He later worked as chief chemist for Thomas Edison and in telegraph research for Westinghouse and the U.S. Weather Service. Efforts to set up in Canada ended when the government opted to subsidize Marconi instead.

Fessenden died in Bermuda in 1932, a genius unsung in his own land.

No statues or monuments, apart from a few plaques, have ever been erected to this brilliant Canadian. No matter. The radio will do.

7

THE QUEEN AND OTHER HIGHNESSES

Mrs. Glucksburg, Regina
What is the Queen's surname? What's the history of the name?
She took the surname Mountbatten upon her marriage in 1947 as
Princess Elizabeth. On the advice of British statesman and historian Sir Winston Churchill, she abandoned the name after ascending
the throne and declared that she and her children would be known
as the "House and Family of Windsor."

Instead of surnames, royals are identified by dynastic names,
often from the estate or territory that formed the founder's power
base.

Because of anti-German feelings during World War I, George V
issued a proclamation in 1917 changing the dynastic name from
Saxe-Coburg to Windsor, after the royal castle which dates back to
William the Conqueror in the 11th century.

While Queen Elizabeth reaffirmed Windsor as the dynastic name
for her and her children, descendants not titled royal highnesses will
bear the surname Mountbatten-Windsor in honor of her husband.

Mountbatten is a family name Prince Philip adopted to get
married. (He needed one to become a British subject).

Compounding the complexity, Mountbatten is an anglicized

alias for Battenberg. But that was his mother's family name. Philip was born a Schleswig-Holstein-Sonderburg-Glucksburg on his dad's side. That's a branch of an even older Royal House, the Oldenbergs.

But in a parallel world where kings and queens were never invented, Lieutenant Philip Glucksburg would have wed Miss Elizabeth Windsor, whose surname had been legally changed from Saxe-Cobourg by her grandfather, and they would live happily ever after.

Royal passports
Do members of the royal family have passports and are they different from ordinary passports?
The Queen does not have a passport because in Britain these are issued in her name. "She would be issuing herself one, basically," is the response from Buckingham Palace.

Other members of her family do have British passports. "They're ordinary passports."

Queen Elizabeth, as Queen of Canada, would not need a passport to come, of course, but what happens when she goes outside the Commonwealth, say, to the U.S. or Russia?

On official visits, she travels on invitation of the host country. But even on a private visit, she'd be formally welcomed and warmly ushered into the country. There are no passport requirements, Buckingham Palace said.

Letter from the Queen
Where do you write to get a letter from the Queen and the Prime Minister for a 50th wedding anniversary?
The Queen's congratulations start with 60th wedding anniversaries and for 100th birthdays. The Governor General responds to 50th wedding anniversaries and 90th birthdays.

Write The Anniversary Section, Office of the Secretary to the Governor General, Government House, Hall, 1 Sussex Drive, Ottawa,

Ont., K1A OA1, about two months in advance of the anniversary. Give full information, typewritten or printed in block letters, on the anniversary, names and address. Documentation on the date of the wedding or birth is required for a message from the Queen.

For the Prime Minister's acknowledgement, write the Prime Minister's office, 90 Wellington St., Ottawa, Ont., K1A 0A2. Mark it: Attention Correspondence Unit.

Oath to head of state

Can I become a Canadian citizen without taking an oath of allegiance to the Queen?

No, says the federal Citizenship Court office in Ottawa. But the goverment's considering leaving the Queen out of it.

Queen on coins

Is the Queen's face on the front or the back of Canadian coins?

She's always on the "obverse," the side of a coin that has the principal design. The other side of the coin is called the "reverse."

Royal titles

When do you use the term, "Your Royal Highness?"

When addressing members of a sovereign's immediate family. But the Queen is "Your Majesty." So is the Queen Mother. She, too, has been anointed in a coronation ceremony.

The others: "All sons and daughters, brothers and sisters, uncles and aunts of the Sovereign are regarded as of the Blood Royal, and designated 'Royal Highness,'" according to *Titled Persons* (1898).

That title also is enjoyed by the wives of Royal Highnesses. And it's the title of the Prince Consort, His Royal Highness Prince Philip, Duke of Edinburgh.

But it's only bestowed on the monarch's grandchildren if they're the offspring of sons. Offspring of daughters, along with nieces, nephews and cousins, are "Highness."

Royal Highness is the title given members of royal families of other countries, as well. But not always. In Monaco, for example, the title is Serene Highness.

Mum as a maiden
What was the Queen Mother's maiden name and how many siblings did she have?

Bowes-Lyon. She was born on August 4, 1900, second youngest of ten children of Claude George Bowes-Lyon, 14th Earl of Strathmore, and Cecilia, daughter of Rev. Charles Cavendish Bentinck. She was baptized Elizabeth Angela Marguerite.

The Queen Mum was born in her father's home at St. Paul's Waldenbury, a village in the west of England. But she always considered herself a Scotswoman through and through. On her father's side, she is a descendant of Robert the Bruce, King of Scotland (1306-1329).

Products fit for a Queen
What does it mean when a product is labelled "by appointment to Her Majesty the Queen"?

Somebody in Buckingham Palace — maybe the Queen, maybe a cook — liked something the company made.

After selling stuff to the palace for three years a firm may apply for a warrant to advertise the fact. A Royal Household Tradesmen's Warrants Committee decides every year who gets one, subject to approval by the Queen, Prince Philip, Prince Charles or the Queen Mother.

The warrant also lets its holder put a royal coat of arms on labels, letterheads, trucks and buildings.

Long live the Queen
Which British monarchs have reigned longer than our Elizabeth II?

Queen Victoria had the longest reign, almost 64 years, 1837 to 1901. Her grandfather, George III ruled for 59 years, 1760 to 1820; Henry

III's reign spanned 56 years, 1216-72; Edward III had half a century, 1327-77; and Elizabeth I lasted almost 45 years, 1558-1603. Queen Elizabeth II acceded to the throne on February 6, 1952, on the death of her father, George VI.

Prince in action
Did Prince Andrew or his unit see any action during the 1982 Falklands War?
Yes. He was thrust into dangerous situations as a 22-year-old Sea King helicopter pilot with 820 Squadron aboard the aircraft carrier *Invincible*, according to press reports from the British fleet at the time.

The Sea Kings' most important jobs were to act as decoys to protect British ships from Exorcet missile attacks, to ferry troops and to conduct anti-submarine sonar patrols in which the helicopters hovered just above whitecaps trailing sensitive sonar microphones in the water.

In one incident, the warship HMS Sheffield was sunk by an Exorcet while Andrew was on a decoy mission nearby, protecting the *Invincible*. "For the first ten minutes after the Sheffield, I think one really didn't know which way to turn or what to do. I knew where I was and I was very frightened then," he told reporters.

The prince had entered the war with the reputation as a playboy and the nickname Randy Andy. He emerged a more thoughtful young man but with zest for life intact.

"Mother of Confederation"
Why do we still celebrate Victoria Day? Did Queen Victoria play a significant part in Canada's history, or what?
She's the "Mother of Confederation," said Garry Toffoli of the Monarchist League of Canada.

He's among those who maintain that without Victoria — the queen as a person and as a symbol — there probably wouldn't be a Canada, at least as we know it.

Toffoli described Victoria as the most Canadian of the royals after her father, Prince Edward, the Duke of Kent, who'd lived in British North America from 1791 to 1801 as its military commander-in-chief.

Though Prince Edward died in her early childhood, Canadian friends continued to visit the family in England and met the young princess as she was growing up. Through them, she acquired an understanding and deep interest in the vast land and its people that continued throughout her reign.

It was in negotiations leading up to Confederation that she played her biggest part in Canadian history. She was actively involved and encouraged John A. Macdonald, George-Étienne Cartier and others in their negotiations, for she believed a united Canada of French and English origin a good idea, similar to one advocated by her father.

Victoria was held in such esteem and affection that among names the fathers proposed for the new confederation were Victorialand and Albertsland, after her husband.

Her name appears more than 300 times on Canadian geographical features, not including cities, towns, institutions, buildings or streets.

Victoria Day, to mark the reigning Queen's birthday, was first proclaimed by the legislature of the Province of Canada in 1845.

The first major celebration, with picnics, fireworks, sports and bands, was held in Toronto in 1849 as a means to counter a manifesto for annexation to the U.S., signed by prominent English Montrealers, upset at compensations won by French Canadians and others after the Rebellion of 1837.

Torontonians, horrified at the thought of annexation, decided to make the Queen's birthday a focus of Canadian independence and loyalty to the crown. The idea of Victoria Day as a statement of Canadian identity and English-French unity spread across the country, Toffoli said.

In 1901, after Victoria's death, the Canadian Parliament, in recognition of her place in Canadian history, declared her birthday to be a memorial holiday.

In Canada, Queen Elizabeth's birthday, which is actually April 21, is officially celebrated on Victoria Day. The holiday has been observed on the first Monday preceding May 25 since 1952.

8

SYMBOLS OF NATIONHOOD

Canada's ancient colors
What do the colors of the Canadian flag represent?

Red and white are the official colors of Canada. "When Canada was granted its coat of arms in 1921, the mantling was red and white and this established the official colors," explained George Stanley, the university dean who designed the maple leaf flag.

Stanley, who later served as New Brunswick's lieutenant-governor, was inspired by the powerful image of the commandant's red and white flag at the Royal Military College in Kingston while developing his ideas.

The white doesn't symbolize snow and red doesn't represent the predominant color of the Canadian landscape in autumn. "Nothing as poetic as that," said Jean-Paul Roy, in charge of ceremonial and protocol for the Canadian Heritage Department in Ottawa. Red and white represent the mother countries of Canada's two founding peoples — background colors of ancient battle flags.

"White has lately been associated with France and red with England. But for centuries earlier on, it was the reverse," Roy said.

Henry V took the French red for the background of his coat of arms after his bloody victory at Agincourt in 1415. Joan of Arc, leading the fight to oust the English, adopted their field of white — a symbol of purity — for France.

Roy put to rest myths that have circulated almost from the time the flag was first hoisted officially February 15, 1965: The 11-point maple leaf doesn't represent the federal government and ten provinces, it's simply an artistic rendering. Nor do the red bars represent seas and white a wintry land between. The flag stands on its own, without myth.

Farewell, old Maple Leaf
What is the proper way to get rid of a Canadian flag that is tattered and torn?
"When a flag becomes worn, noticeably faded or otherwise unfit for service, it should be disposed of privately by burning," according to Arms, Flags and Emblems of Canada and Heritage Canada.

"Burning is the only way to do it," added Alan Boothe, owner of Dominion Regalia Ltd. in Toronto, maker of flags since 1881. "Burn it till only ashes are left. Another thing, you burn it in private. Doing it in public is not honoring the flag."

Order of honor
Is it possible to nominate someone for the Order of Canada?
Go ahead. The Order of Canada is described as "a fraternity of merit, not a society of the elite." It is the centerpiece of the Canadian system of honors. Its object is to pay tribute to people who in their lives and work exemplify the greatest qualities of citizenship and enrich the lives of others. Its motto, in Latin, is: "They desire a better country."

Nominations are received by The Chancellery, Rideau Hall, Ottawa, Ont., K1A 0A1. A letter will do, but a nomination form is available from the Chancellery. The nomination should be accompanied by a biographical sketch, setting out the person's career and achievements. Personal testimony of close associates is really helpful, Chancellery staff said.

An advisory council, chaired by the Chief Justice of Canada, assesses nominations and recommends the names of those considered most worthy to the governor general, the order's chancellor.

The badge is a stylized snowflake bearing the crown, a maple leaf and the motto.

Membership is at three levels: the Companion level recognizes international service or achievement, or national pre-eminence; the Officer level recognizes national service or achievement, and the Member level recognizes outstanding contributions that are local or regional in scope.

Symbolism and a flag
What was Newfoundland's flag before it joined Canada?

The British Union Jack, which had flown over The Rock since early in the 19th century, was adopted by statute as Newfoundland's official flag in 1931. After the 1949 union with Canada, it flew as the provincial flag for three decades.

Other flags had flown throughout Newfoundland's recorded history, probably beginning with the Viking's raven flag a millennium ago. In the late 1800s, a pink, white and green flag, the united banner of two St. John's societies, was known as the "native flag," but never officially adopted.

Newfoundland's flag today is of geometric design — reminiscent of the crosses of the Union Jack — on a white background, adopted by the legislative assembly in 1980. The flag has four blue triangles near the staff and a gold arrow between two red-outlined triangles in the fly.

Much symbolism has been read into it. Here's how it's described in a circular from the province's ministry of culture and tourism: the two red triangles represent the island and Labrador mainland. White represents snow, blue the sea and Commonwealth heritage. Large red and gold areas represent human effort and confidence, and the arrow points the way to the future.

And there's more. If you look closely, the ministry advises, a maple leaf is outlined in the center. The image of a trident also stands out, representing the province's dependence on resources of the sea. The arrow becomes a sword when the flag is hung as a banner.

But these interpretations didn't come from the flag's creator, Newfoundland painter Christopher Pratt. He intended no overt symbolism. "People read in symbolism after the fact," he said.

Two principles did guide him in the design, though. The angles were meant to suggest the three crosses that make up the Union Jack. "That was very deliberate. A lot of people here wanted to retain the Union Jack in the provincial flag and some did not. This was my attempt to compromise," he said.

The other source of the triangles comes from ornamentation of Newfoundland's original Naskapi and Beothuk peoples. It's as simple as that. After all, he said, "What is a flag? A flag basically is a piece of cloth by which you know your friends so you don't shoot them in the ass."

There's no mistaking a Newfoundlander under Pratt's flag.

From sea even unto sea

What does the Latin in the Canadian coat of arms mean? I've forgotten what *usque* means.

Canada's motto is *A Mari Usque Ad Mare*, which is officially translated as "From Sea to Sea" in English and *D'un ocean a l'autre* in French.

Literal translations incorporating *usque* might be "from sea even unto sea" or "from sea also unto sea."

The motto in Latin was formally added to Canada's armorial bearings in 1921 and comes from the eighth verse of the 72nd Psalm: *Et dominabitur a mari usque ad mare, et a flumine ad terminos obis terrarum.* The authorized version in English: "He shall have dominion also from sea to sea, and from the river unto the ends of the earth."

Canada's political colors
Why Conservative blue and Liberal red? Why isn't the New Democratic Party associated with a color?

In Canada, blue and red party colors appeared in Quebec about the middle of the 19th century.

The Parti bleu, made up of Quebec moderates, was in the coalition welded into the modern Conservative party by Sir John A. Macdonald about the time of Confederation. And by that time, blue was already associated with Conservatives in Britain.

Quebec's Parti rouge reformers and Ontario's Clear Grits merged to form the Liberal party in 1873. Red was the color of choice for reformers and radicals. Rouges and Grits enjoyed those labels. British Liberals earlier adopted blue and yellow.

The New Democratic Party color is orange, chosen after its founding in 1961. It's sometimes used with green, brown or black. "They wanted something different. It was pleasant. It was visible," said Donald MacDonald, patriarch of the Ontario NDP and its leader from 1952 to 1979. "They adopted it in an effort to get, particularly in city ridings, each candidate using the same color on election signs."

Green is the Reform party color. "As I recall, when we chose the color, it had to do with green in terms of new growth, a new beginning ... It's almost a spring green," said Ron Wood of party leader Preston Manning's office.

Fragile emblem
Is it illegal to pick a white trillium, Ontario's floral emblem, in the province?

In general, no, say officials with the Attorney General's ministry and the Ministry of Natural Resources. But don't pick the three-leaved, three-petalled flower in provincial parks, where it is forbidden by law to destroy flora, or on private property, where you could be charged for trespassing.

Think about this, though, before you pick the flower: a trillium seed takes six years to produce a healthy root and develop into a full-grown plant capable of producing a flower.

The folks at the Kortright Centre for Conservation near Toronto say picking the flowers removes the leaves, the food producing part of the trillium, starving the rootstock and killing the plant.

Canada's national songs
Was there a national anthem before "O Canada" and, if so, what was it called?

Before Parliament proclaimed "O Canada" the national anthem in 1967, it was one of three or four national songs sung or played on public occasions.

The first was the royal anthem, "God Save the Queen," which is also recognized as Britain's national anthem by virtue of popular feeling over almost two centuries, though not in legislation.

The second was "The Maple Leaf Forever," written by Toronto schoolmaster Alexander Muir in 1867, but not particularly popular in Quebec, because of its strong anglo point of view ("Wolfe, the dauntless hero").

Another often heard was "Rule Britannia," but it was hardly popular among those across the country who had nationalist stirrings.

Aside from "O Canada," Quebecers preferred their own vigorous and informal *chants national*, many of them as light-hearted as "Vive la Canadienne."

Pro-British patriotic song
You don't hear it much any more, but I was wondering, what are the words to "The Maple Leaf Forever?"

A couple of lines of the patriotic song are sometimes altered to soften a pro-British tone unacceptable to French Canadians, who'd been first to adopt the maple leaf as a national symbol anyway.

The original opening verses, including chorus, written in October 1867, by Muir, who was inspired by a maple leaf that fell on him during a stroll around Leslie Park:

In days of yore, from Britain's shore,
Wolfe, the dauntless hero, came
And planted firm Britainnia's flag
On Canada's fair domain.

Here may it wave, our boast and pride,
And joined in love together,
The Thistle, Shamrock, Rose entwine
The Maple Leaf forever!

The Maple Leaf, our emblem dear,
The Maple Leaf forever;
God save our Queen, and Heaven bless
The Maple Leaf forever.

Among later changes is inclusion of the French lily in a line that
reads:

With Lilly (*sic.*), Thistle, Shamrock, Rose,
The Maple Leaf forever.

The Maple Leaf flag was adopted by Parliament on October 22,
1964, and proclaimed by Queen Elizabeth on February 15, 1965.

9

PLANET CANADA

'Cold' blue for recycling
Why are blue boxes blue rather than another color, say, environmental green?

Don Holliday, president of A-1 Products Corp., the Milton, Ont., firm that developed the recycling box marketing strategy in the mid-1980s, explained: "Blue is a very high-profile color and is considered to be a 'cold' rather than a 'warm' color.

"What that means is blue is going to stand out on the curb in any weather and in any season. You want people to see the boxes as they drive by and reinforce the message of recycling."

In testing colors for the boxes, the company found green boxes tended to blend in with lawns and shrubs. Other colors tested were also rejected.

"Cold colors stand out. They're almost abrasive. They jump out at you. ... Because blue does not fit into many decorating situations, it stands out and, again, reinforces the 'let's recycle' message," Holliday explained.

Canada warms over the century
Is global warming really happening? It seems to me it's getting colder, not warmer.
Canada's air temperature warmed by 1.1 Celsius degrees between 1895 and 1991, an Environment Canada study determined. It traced a warming trend from the 1890s to the 1940s, a cooling from the 1940s to the 1970s and a resumption in the warming in the late 1970s.

"The 1980s were indisputably the warmest decade on record," a report on the study found. Average air temperatures warmed the most in central Canada, up to 1.5°C in some areas.

The trends are similar to those observed globally, the report said, and are "consistent with predictions of global warming as a result of human-caused increases in greenhouse gases."

U.S. and European scientists reported the years 1995 and 1991 were the Earth's warmest on record. That the trends appear to be accelerating are shown in various projections, including those from a two-year study by the National Academy of Sciences in the United States. Five huge computer simulations, "general circulation models," indicate a temperature increase on a global average in the range of one and five Celsius degrees by 2040, said Rob Coppock, who was the academy's staff officer for the study, which involved scientists across the United States.

The lowest increases will be at the equator, rising perhaps 12 degrees higher at the poles, studies suggest.

According to the greenhouse-effect theory, less of the sun's energy is radiated back into space because more of it is absorbed in the atmosphere by the carbon dioxide build-up from the burning of fossil fuels during two centuries of industrialization.

Recycling liquor bottles
Why aren't liquor and wine bottles recycled? Beer bottles are.
Unlike Brewers' Retail Inc., which deals in a limited number of beer bottle shapes, primarily domestic bottles, liquor and wine bottles come in all shapes and sizes from more than 50 countries. "It makes

it very complex to deal with a container recovery system," said Chris Layton of the Liquor Control Board of Ontario.

But they're looking at it. A consulting firm has studied several options, including an expanded municipal blue box program. Other options are returning bottles to depots or liquor stores for recycling or for refilling.

Blue box programs, from which glass is sold for crushing and recycling, are by far the most economical. "To implement any of the other solutions would require huge amounts of money," said John Pendyk, the LCBO's co-ordinator of environmental management. Cost isn't the only obstacle to refillable bottles.

"The only way distillers in Canada can market their products is to have distinctive bottle shapes because they can't advertise on TV," he said. "The logistics of trying to segregate all the Crown Royal bottles, for example, and send them back to the distiller would be insurmountable."

Also, reusable domestic bottles would be at a disadvantage on shelves next to shiny new foreign bottles. Pendyk talked to Canadian wine industry officials about that. "They've really made great strides in the past five years, and they were saying, "The last thing we need is to have ugly-looking bottles, all scuffed up, on our shelves.'"

Elm survivors
Are there any elm trees left? They were ravaged by disease a few years back.

While forests of American (or white) elms were devastated in the 1950s and 1960s by Dutch elm disease, a fungus spread by the elm bark beetle, Winnipeg's trees are mostly elms and many pockets of older trees are found throughout central Canada along with young trees planted since the infestation.

"It didn't wipe out elms 100 per cent. Some of the trees in the middle of hugely infected areas survived," said Professor D. N. Roy, wood chemistry specialist in the forestry faculty at the University of Toronto.

In the early 1970s, Roy developed a chemical, marketed under the trade name Lignasan, now used world-wide to immunize the trees against Dutch elm disease. "There are quite a few (elms) on campus, which were injected by my chemical years ago," Roy said.

The umbrella-shaped elms are also found in Toronto's Don Valley and across ravines, cemeteries and on private property, and are the main shade trees of places like Regina. Elms are the best-suited shade trees on the prairie and withstand the intense cold of winter, Roy said.

But pathologist Martin Hubbes of the U of T's forestry faculty found signs in Toronto's Don Valley that Dutch elm disease has flared up again and he expected, "We will see even more elms dying, young elms."

Hubbes is involved in a three-prong effort to control the disease. He seeks to: develop elms resistant to the disease; prevent its spread by the elm bark beetle, and block the activity of the gene that produces the toxin killing the trees.

The disease, which clogs the elm's water-conducting mechanisms, first appeared in the U.S. in the 1930s and was spotted in Sorel, Que., a decade later, Roy said. But Dutch elm disease spread into Ontario through New York state and the Detroit area. It almost wiped out elms in Windsor and ravaged stands everywhere.

Autumn leaves
Why do leaves change color in the autumn?
Strictly speaking, the leaves don't really change color. Yellow, red and purple pigments were always there. We just couldn't see them for the chlorophyll, the green coloring matter of the leaves, which in sunlight converts water and carbon dioxide into food for the tree.

The shorter days and cool nights of autumn cause the chlorophyll to break down and the hidden colors show. The color of the leaf depends on which of the other pigments is most plentiful in a type of tree.

Masked urban neighbors
What's the raccoon population in urban areas?

Well, about 10,000 of the critters dwell in Metro Toronto, Canada's most populated urban center. That's about eight to 16 raccoons per square kilometre (0.38 square mile), said research scientist Richard Rosatte, the Ontario Ministry of Natural Resources' raccoon specialist.

But in forested areas of a metropolis, such as the Toronto Hunt Club overlooking Lake Ontario in Scarborough, surveys showed about 85 raccoons per square kilometre.

Typical urban habitats are ravines, dug-in areas, shaded areas, and openings in roofs or crawl spaces under houses — places that are cool and dark and difficult for humans to reach.

Moose racks
Do moose lose their antlers?

Yes, every winter. Bulls start growing them again in early spring. They're fully grown by late summer, ready for strutting and fighting during the mating season.

Days of darkness
Why was it completely dark from noon until about 6 p.m. on September 24, 1950?

Would you believe the curse of Daylight Saving Time darkened the world? That's what some people thought. Others believed it was an atomic explosion or aliens from outer space, even the end of the world. No kidding.

Day became night over central Canada and large areas of the U.S. during four days of weird, purplish skies and "celestial upheavals."

A streaking meteorite exploded into three pieces as darkness descended. Fowl roosted early and cows lowed for milking. The first measurable September snow in 100 years fell. It didn't completely clear until after an eclipse of the harvest moon.

The cause — as in similar dark "doomsdays," such as the Black

Friday of May 19, 1780 — was a great pall of smoke 240 kilometres (150 miles) wide and more than 600 metres (2,000 feet) thick from 40 forest and muskeg fires raging in northern Alberta. Freakish winds carried it 3,200 kilometres (2,000 miles) into eastern Canada and the U.S.

The next day, *The Toronto Star* reported: "Some citizens thought the end of the world had come and prayed in terror. Many blamed the purple cloud on an atomic explosion.

Citizens saw flying saucers and a bursting sun. Some said a supernatural power was angry with the world for tampering with Daylight Saving Time."

10

LOVE A COLD CLIMATE

Cold, coldest capitals
Is Ottawa the coldest capital in the world?

If you're talking about the weather, no. Depending on how you measure the temperatures, Ottawa is second or third coldest, said David Phillips, senior climatologist with Environment Canada's Atmospheric Environment Service.

Easily the coldest is Ulan Bator, capital of the Mongolian People's Republic. Its average January temperature — the daily highs and lows for the month over 30 years — is -26°C (-15°F). Its average annual temperature is -3°C (27°F).

Next is Ottawa and/or Moscow. Phillips calls them "climatic twins." The average January temperature in Ottawa is -10.9°C (12.4°F). In Moscow it's -10.3°C (13.5°F). January is the coldest month of the year in both capitals.

But July is warmer in Ottawa than in Moscow and in year-round average temperatures, Moscow is fractionally colder than Ottawa. No other capital in the northern or southern hemisphere is colder than those three, Phillips said.

Canada is truly the Great White North, the second coldest country in the world with an average annual temperature of -4.4°C. We used to be Number One, but with the break-up of the Soviet Union and the shedding of southerly republics, Russia comes in with a yearly average temperature of -5.3°C. A distant third is Outer Mongolia, at -0.7°C.

Happy groundhogwash day

How accurate is the myth that if the groundhog sees its shadow on February 2, there'll be another six weeks of winter?

A ten-year study of weather records in Toronto by Environment Canada showed groundhogs were only right 30 per cent of the time. You'd get better odds flipping a coin.

According to the legend brought to the New World by early settlers, the groundhog awakens from its winter's sleep on February 2. If the sun is shining, the animal is startled by its shadow and crawls back into its hole, which means six more weeks of winter ahead. If the day is cloudy, the groundhog stays out, a sign that spring is around the corner. Climatologist Bryan Smith of Environment Canada's Ontario Climate Centre, said, "I used to call it 'groundhogwash' because there's not much to it. But mainly it's just for fun. February is such a boring month for a lot of people."

Canada dry

Where is the driest climate in Canada? I suffer from arthritis in this damp climate.

Low pressure and high humidity together are the most debilitating weather for arthritis sufferers, according to studies carried out in climate chambers where pressure, temperature and humidity were controlled.

So climatologist Phillips, who's also a writer and broadcaster on weather issues, came up with lists of places that enjoy low humidity and generally high pressure, mostly in southeastern British Columbia and southern Alberta.

But he advised people who are weather-sensitive to, "Go visit a location not just once but in all seasons so that you get a sense of what it is really like."

Kamloops is driest in terms of relative humidity, with mid-afternoon readings year-round averaging 52 per cent. In Toronto, it averages 65 per cent. It's much drier in U.S. desert areas: a relative humidity of 25 per cent in Las Vegas on average in April.

Lowest annual precipitation in Canada is in the Arctic. Eureka, N.W.T. gets 64 millimetres a year. That's just over two inches, less than they get in U.S. deserts, such as 114 mm in Las Vegas. Only Death Valley has less — 41 mm of precipitation a year.

In more comfortable climes, Kamloops gets 238 millimetres of precipitation in an average year. Penticton has 265 millimetres. Metro Toronto has 781 millimetres. Kenora, with 569 to 623 mm of precipitation, has the lowest annual precipitation in Ontario.

Medicine Hat, Alta., has the most days without precipitation, averaging 271 days a year. It's 265 days in Lethbridge, Alta., and 263 in Kamloops. In Toronto, the average is 224 days in a year without rain.

Compare that with Phoenix, Arizona, with 325 days, or 354 days in Death Valley, Calif. But who'd want to live there?

U.S. vs Canadian barometers

I have a barometer made in the U.S. and the units are in inches, presumably of mercury. How can I get the equivalent in kilopascals, as given out in Canadian weather reports?

The conversion factor is 3.387. Multiply your barometer's readings by 3.387 to get kilopascals.

A pascal is a unit for measuring pressure. A kilopascal (kPa) is 1,000 pascals. The standard pressure of the atmosphere at sea level is 101.32 kPa at 0°C. That's equal to 14.7 pounds per square inch, which will support a column of mercury almost 30 inches high.

If our arithmetic is correct, 101.32 kPa is 29.91 inches. Metro Toronto averages 101.58 kPa year-round (converted to sea level) or 29.99 inches.

To convert kilopascals to the equivalent in inches, divide by 3.387.

A ton of air above us
Why aren't we crushed to death by air pressure of 15 pounds per square inch at sea level?

In fact, the average person supports about a ton of air, said Lucy Warner at the U.S. National Centre for Atmospheric Research in Boulder, Colo.

Some days, it sure feels like it.

"We're not crushed because an equal force is pushing outward from inside our bodies," she said. "It's pushing in all directions, not just from above — it's pushing up, down, sideways and outwards from inside. It's an equalized force, inside your body and outside your body."

Our bodies aren't sealed like, say, a plastic bottle of soda pop, said physicist Sudhakar Joshi of York University. We breathe. Our skin is porous. There's air inside us.

If we took a plastic bottle to a mountain top, emptied it and recapped it, we'd find back at sea level the bottle slightly squashed. That's because air pressure outside the bottle at sea level is greater than the pressure inside the bottle when we capped it on the mountain.

But we're fine, of course. Our unsealed bodies adjusted to the difference in atmospheric pressure as we came down.

For the record, the pressure in Metro Toronto, measured at Pearson International Airport at 173 metres above sea level, averages 99.5 kilopascals, or 14.43 pounds per square inch.

Winds of winter wilder
Why is there more wind in wintertime than in summer?

Winds are created by unequal temperatures on the surface of the earth and air pressure. Warmer air is usually low pressure and rises. Colder air rushes in as wind to replace it.

Winter winds seem particularly harsh in southern Ontario. "We're in the middle of the battleground between cold Arctic air and warm gulf air from the south," explained Bryan Smith at the Ontario Climate Centre.

In summer, the battleground shifts further north as the Arctic air retreats.

Greater differences in temperature occur in winter than in summer, he said. In this part of the world, temperatures run from 10° to -30° Celsius in winter, a difference of 40 degrees.

Summer temperatures normally run between 10° and 30° Celsius, a difference of 20 degrees.

Squeaky snow
Why does snow squeak when we walk on it? The colder it is, the more it squeaks.

We're probably hearing ice crystals bump and grind, but there are other theories.

One explanation is that when the temperature is a little below freezing, your pressure compresses and melts the snow. So, no noise is created.

But when the temperature is well below freezing, say minus 20, the snow can't melt when you step on it. It yields abruptly as the crushed ice crystals slip over and crush into each other. The sudden rubbing, slipping or smashing of the dry, separated crystals produce that familiar cold-weather creaking.

Another factor possibility: the pressure of stepping on the air-filled snowflakes rapidly expels the air and produces the characteristic squeak.

Quaqtak's tourist problem
What's the windiest place in Canada? In the world?

An hourly average wind speed of 201 kilometres (125 mph) per hour was recorded in what is now Quaqtak in Quebec's Ungava Peninsula on November 19, 1931.

For windy cities, try St. John's, Nfld., where the average measured over two decades was 24.3 km/h (15 mph), with gusts of up to 193 km/h (120 mph).

In Toronto, the average was 18 km/h (11 mph) but on January 26, 1978, a gale gusted to 126 km/h (78 mph) on the Toronto Islands.

Folklore suggests the windiest place in Canada is the intersection of Portage and Main in downtown Winnipeg. But Winnipeg's 20-year average was 18.6 km/h (11.5 mph), just a puff above Toronto's. (By the way, Chicago got the nickname "the windy city" because of its voluble politicians).

The world's strongest wind speed was recorded on Mount Washington in New Hampshire on April 12, 1934, at 362 km/h (225 mph). Over a five-minute period, the wind averaged 303 km/h (188 mph).

No one knows of gusts above 362 km/h. At that speed, wind-measuring equipment gets blown away.

The windiest place in the world is Antarctica, where storms produce gusts along the George V Coast as high as 320 km/h (200 mph).

A number of Canadian places have names that relate to wind, The Canadian Press has noted, including Blizzard Point, Nfld., Blow Me Down, Nfld., Cape Storm, N.W.T., Chinook, Alta., Lac Storm, Que., Snowdrift, N.W.T., Tornado Mountain, Alta.-B.C., Wind River, Yukon, Windygates, Man., Windy Mouth, B.C., and Zephyr, Ont.

When tornadoes strike

What are the chances of a tornado this far north and what precautions should I take?

About 75 tornadoes — 25 in Ontario alone — touch down in Canada every season, roughly April through October. Keep an ear to your radio during severe weather watches issued by Environment Canada. Tornadoes may accompany severe thunderstorms.

Here are some suggestions about what to do if a tornado strikes:

Stay away from windows, doors and outside walls; protect your head; go to either the center of your building or the side farthest from the storm; avoid arenas, barns, supermarkets and other structures with unsupported roofs if a tornado warning is issued; in such structures seek the lowest floor, an inside hallway, a windowless interior room, or duck under something sturdy; in the open, move at right angles from a tornado's direction or, if it turns on you, find a ditch or ravine and lie flat; grab a small tree or shrub if no other shelter is available; never try to ride it out in a vehicle.

Toronto's climate

Can you tell me what Metro Toronto's climate is called? I'm shivering in anticipation.

That depends on which geographer you ask, said Smith, at Environment Canada's Ontario Climate Centre. He described it as a "modified continental climate" because the Great Lakes' influence keeps it from getting as hot or as cold as it could.

Morley Thomas, historian for the weather service, called it a "humid and temperate continental climate." The "humid" means Toronto is not as arid as the continent's western provinces and states, and "temperate" means it doesn't get as cold for as long as it does in our north, he said.

Computer projections say global warming will heat the planet by between two and three degrees Celsius over the next 50 years. "As the greenhouse effect develops, the climate of Toronto will approach a climate similar to Cincinnati or Indianapolis," Smith said. That means milder winters and warmer summers. But not that warm: "No palm trees — or alligators — in the Don River," he said.

The climate has shown some wide extremes in the more than 150 years of national weather service daily observations.

For the record, here are some of the high and low marks: Toronto's hottest day: 40.6° Celsius (105° Fahrenheit), July 10, 1936; coldest day: -32.8°C (-27°F), January 10, 1859; warmest summer: 1949's mean temperature of 22.8°C (73°F); coldest winter: 1874-75, with a mean temperature of -8.5°C (17°F); snowiest winter: 1869-70, with 314 centimetres (10 feet, four inches) of snow; winter with least snow: 1952-53, 47 centimetres (19 inches); snowiest day: 48.3 centimetres (19 inches) on December 11, 1944; sunniest year: 1978 had 2,323 hours of sunshine; rainiest year: 1843, with 1,308 millimetres (51 inches); rainiest day: 98.6 millimetres (3.9 inches) on July 27, 1897. The tremendous thunderstorm that day left more rain in a 24-hour period than Hurricane Hazel, which deposited 96.2 millimetres (3.8 inches) on October 15, 1954. Hazel also lashed Toronto with 5.8 millimetres of rain the night before; highest wind gust: 126 km/h (36 km/h over the speed limit on the Gardiner Expressway) on January 26, 1978, on the Toronto Islands, during a storm blowing off Lake Ontario.

Bring a coat.

Sunny Saskatchewan
What is the sunniest city or town in Canada?

Estevan, Sask., with an annual 2,537 hours, says Environment Canada. In central and eastern Canada, 2,300 hours of sunshine would be a record year.

Rainy Saskatchewan
What was the heaviest rainfall ever recorded in Canada?

A total of 250 millimetres (ten inches) fell in under an hour at Buffalo Gap, Sask., on May 30, 1961. Heavy hail and strong winds eroded fields and stripped bark from large trees, the Canadian Weather Calendar says.

Hot Saskatchewan
What is the warmest city in Canada? What was the highest temperature in Canada?

The highest temperature ever recorded in Canada was 45°C (113°F) in Midale, Sask., on July 5, 1937. But taking the mean annual temperature, the warmest place is Sumas Canal in southwestern British Columbia at 10.7°C (51.3°F). The warmest city is Victoria, B.C., with its mean annual temperature of 10.4°C (50.7°F).

Cold Alert
What is Canada's northernmost weather station?
Alert, located on Ellesmere Island, about 750 kilometres (466 miles) from the North Pole; it's the most northerly one in the world. Alert is a military base. But Environment Canada weather observers and scientists are also there.

Fr-fr-fr-frigid
What is the coldest temperature ever recorded in Canada?
The lowest temperature was minus 63°C (minus 81°F), recorded in Snag, Yukon, February 3, 1947.

Reporting records
Weather records from the past are given in Celsius in the newspapers. Weren't they in Fahrenheit 50 and 100 years ago?
Temperature records, which were in Fahrenheit before Canada introduced the metric system in 1973, are converted to Celsius readings for use in today's weather reports.

11

HOUSE ON THE HILL

Shhh, teachers told MPs

When did the tradition of parliamentary desk-thumping start? Why has it now been replaced by applause?

Desk-thumping to express enthusiasm became a noisy Canadian tradition after the introduction of desks in the country's legislatures. Desks were installed with the benches in the Commons chamber when the original Parliament Buildings opened in Ottawa in 1866, archival material shows.

The din petered out on Parliament Hill more than a century later. For one thing, MPs' former school teachers didn't like it.

Clapping was first heard — aside from occasional derisive applause — from Conservative benches in the fall of 1978, mentions in Hansard, the Parliamentary record, show. But applause didn't really begin to replace thumping until after the introduction in 1979 of televised proceedings by nation-wide satellite hook-up.

A significant number of Canadians received broad exposure to goings on in the House, and shortly after, members started receiving a fairly steady stream of letters — "many of them, I'm told, from their former school teachers," said Bob Desramaux, director-general of information technologies, head of the parliamentary broadcasting service.

The desks have a hinged top, like old-style school desks, and under the lid is storage space. "It was not pounding on the desks with their hands necessarily, but grabbing the edge and whacking it up and down to make noise," Desramaux said.

Viewers complained the members were behaving like a bunch of rowdy pupils and, besides, all that noise on the television audio made it hard to hear what was going on. The experience of one MP was typical. What really got to him was when his sixth-grade teacher wrote to him and said, "You know, I would never have you behave like that in my classroom."

"And fairly quickly the consensus was that applauding was more seemly and thumping just gradually faded away," Desramaux said.

Clapping in Canadian legislatures started in Quebec in 1976 after the separatist Parti Quebecois came to power. The PQ adopted the polite practice of France's National Assembly.

In Parliament, MPs initially resisted clapping. Hansard quotes New Democrat MP Arnold Peters on October 29, 1979, saying applause gave Canada "a French accent" and "changed our ways ... to correspond to the ways of France."

But desk-thumping is not a British tradition. They don't have desks in the Mother of Parliaments at Westminster, Desramaux noted. They don't clap there either.

Sharp shoes
What is the history behind the tradition of Canadian finance ministers wearing new shoes when they present the budget?
Someone either pulled Mitchell Sharp's leg, or was badly misinformed.

Sharp, finance minister in the Liberal government in 1966-67 was the first to don new shoes for budget night. "Inadvertently," he said.

Someone — he doesn't remember who — told him finance ministers traditionally wear new shoes when presenting the budget. "So I accepted that at face value and bought a good pair of shoes

(Canadian-made, about $40) that I wore budget night. Later, I learned there was no tradition behind it at all."

That's what the research branch of the Parliamentary Library in Ottawa discovered, too. Researchers queried finance ministers back to World War II, and poured over Hansard, literature and press clippings to earlier eras hoping to track the budget-night shoes to their source.

All trails led to Sharp's shoe closet and the mysterious adviser.

The British hadn't started it. They have an interesting habit of their own. Westminster tradition allows the Chancellor of the Exchequer to carry into the House an "old dispatch box" containing any liquid refreshment of his own choosing to quench thirst while delivering the budget speech.

Since Sharp's day, dozens of provincial finance ministers and most federal finance ministers have purchased new shoes for budget night.

The five other federal ministers of finance who've worn new shoes to present their budgets were Liberal Jean Chrétien, Conservative John Crosbie, Liberal Marc Lalonde, Conservative Michael Wilson and Liberal Paul Martin, who donned new work boots to deliver his deficit-cutting budget in 1995.

Conservative Don Mazankowski wore a new tie instead for his first budget in February 1992. As a symbol, it was bad luck. The electorate lynched the party the following year.

Honorable in politics
Who in Canada are titled "Honorable" or "Right Honorable"?
Prime ministers have been automatically styled Right Honorable since 1968. They keep the title for life. Members of the federal cabinet and other members of the Queen's Privy Council of Canada get to be Honorable for life.

The Speaker of the House of Commons is Honorable while in office and, afterwards, on appointment to the privy council by the governor general.

Senators are Honorable for as long as they live.

Governors general have the title Right Honorable for life, and so do chief justices of Canada. The serving G G and spouse also have the title excellency while in office, as in: His Excellency the Right Honorable Romeo LeBlanc.

Judges of the Supreme Court of Canada, the Federal Court and Tax Court of Canada, and those on provincial high courts, county and district courts are styled Honorable while in office. They may receive permission from the governor general, on behalf of the Queen, to retain the title after leaving office.

A provincial lieutenant-governor keeps the title Honorable for life. While in office, they also have the title, shared with spouse, of Your Honor. Speakers of the legislatures and cabinet ministers are Honorable while in office.

Advisers to the Queen
Who are members of the privy council?

The Queen's Privy Council for Canada is a body of advisers to the crown, appointed for life by the governor general, and its working part is the prime minister and his cabinet. They are the "committee of council," and act under the authority of the crown in the conduct of state business through orders-in-council issued by the governor general. Other members of the privy council are the Chief Justice of Canada, the Leader of the Official Opposition, former governors general, former speakers of the House of Commons and Senate, former clerks of the privy council and, of course, former prime ministers and cabinet ministers and chief justices. So is the Prince Consort, Philip, Duke of Edinburgh.

Provincial premiers were appointed members during Confederation Year in 1967, and so were premiers who participated in the 1982 patriation of the Constitution. They remain members as long as they live.

Appointed to the privy council in the past have been individuals with exceptionally devoted and meritorious service to Parliament and the Crown, such as senators David Croll and Eugene Forsey before their deaths.

"Honorary members" have also been appointed.

Privy council origins go back to at least 11th-century England and William the Conqueror, who met in his private chambers with trusted advisers.

The Privy Council for Canada was established in 1867, but apart from cabinet functions, its role is a formal or ceremonial one. It last met in full in 1981. That was to formally recognize the Queen's consent to the marriage of Charles, the Prince of Wales.

Parliamentary nest eggs
What kind of pension would MPs get?

That depends on when they were elected. Under reforms in 1995, the parliamentary pension plan covers three situations to ensure the retirement years of long-time members of Parliament are golden. The original is for those who retired before 1995, another is for those who'll be elected from then on, and a third covers those whose terms spanned 1995.

To figure out the pension of an MP who retired before 1995, multiply years in office (maximum allowed for pension purposes is 15 years) by 5 per cent. Then multiply that by the average of the six best-paid years in office.

More than 400 former members of the House of Commons currently draw this pension. To qualify, they must have served at least six years. For full benefits, they must have paid 11 per cent of earnings into the parliamentary pension plan under the Members of Parliament Retiring Allowances Act.

Say a 45-year-old MP retired in 1993 after ten years in office, having contributed the maximum 11 per cent into the plan.

Public records would show the MP's pay during the six years leading up to retirement in 1963 averaged out to $62,333 (a $21,300 tax-free allowance isn't figured in). With ten years' service in the House of Commons, the ex-MP would draw a pension of 50 per cent of the $62,333, which is $31,166.50 a year.

Cabinet ministers, earning a total of $113,500, do better, based on their higher income.

But a prime minister's situation is treated differently than other members. He or she gets a full pension as an MP, but the pension on the PM supplement must wait till 65. He or she will then be paid two-thirds of whatever the prime minister's supplement is at that time, provided up to 7 per cent of the PM supplement has been paid into the plan.

For example, public records show that over Brian Mulroney's last six years in the House, his pay on the MP portion of his salary averaged out to $62,333. With ten years of service in the Commons, he'd be entitled to a pension of $31,166.50 a year, 50 per cent of MPs' pay.

Getting back to the humble backbencher also with ten years in the House, a pension cheque of $2,597 arrives monthly, on top of any salary earned in the private sector.

But if the former MP (or PM, too) has a federal appointment, the pension will be reduced by the amount of their earnings in excess of $5,000. This ending of "double dipping" was the only impact on this category of retiree of the 1995 parliamentary pension reforms.

The reforms still allow parliamentary pensions to become fully indexed to the cost of living at age 60. They're also adjusted then to reflect the accumulated impact of inflation since retirement.

Should our ex-backbencher live to age 75, pension payments would total well over $1 million — *how* well over depends on inflation.

Since the 1995 reforms, the new minimum pensionable age for MPs first elected in 1993 will be 55.

Their pensions will be based on 4 per cent for every year of service up to 19 years, rather than 5 per cent over 15 years. They now pay 9 per cent of their salary a year toward the pension plan, rather than 11 per cent.

The current provisions apply only to that portion of members' pension after enactment of the 1995 amendment to retiring allowances act.

That means he or she will collect fully on pensions paid into the scheme prior to the 1995 reforms upon leaving the Commons. The part of the pensions affected by the reforms kick in at age 55. But this too becomes fully indexed to inflation at age 60.

The government expected the reforms to reduce its annual contribution to the parliamentary pension plan from about $10 million to $6.7 million a year, a drop of $3.3 million.

MPs also pay into the Canada Pension Plan and, at age 65, qualify for Old Age Security, same as other Canadians.

On the bright side, their pensions, like lottery jackpots in the United States, are taxable.

Minor parties on the Hill
In Parliament, what does loss of official party status mean?

Under the Parliament of Canada Act, a political party having at least 12 members elected to the House of Commons is an official party.

Trouble is, the act doesn't say what happens to a party that has had fewer than 12 elected. Such was the predicament of the two Progressive Conservatives and nine New Democrats in office after the dust settled following the 1993 election. What they found was nothing good happens.

In the absence of rules, the standing of such groups traditionally has been decided through negotiations among all parties, for example, during meetings of House leaders. The government side would carry most weight, naturally.

Usually, minor parties were denied official status. This means leaders of unofficial parties have no guarantee they'll be recognized by the Speaker during Question Period, and members are usually last in line for committee seats. Also, the leaders aren't paid the stipend given other leaders.

Until the 1960s, this didn't mean much since all MPs are considered equal. But in the early 1960s, research funds were first made available to "official parties."

Research funds are the major reward, worth hundreds of thousands of dollars. The amounts are determined by the Commons board of internal economy, headed by the Speaker, after all parties have had their say. The money pays for research staff hired by a party to investigate any issue — social, economic, cultural and so on — its MPs wish to raise.

But seldom do minor parties get a piece of this, as the Conservatives and New Democrats discovered. After the all-party discussions, research office allotments meted out after the 1993 election were: Liberal government $1,349,000; Bloc Quebecois Official Opposition $851,000; Reform, the second party in Opposition $826,000.

What did the New Democrats and Conservatives get? Zilch.

Research allotments for the previous Parliament that followed the 1988 election were: Conservative government, $1,348,700; Liberals, as the Official Opposition, $1,095,800; and the NDP, $765,300. The Bloc Quebecois, with eight seats, and the Reform party, with one, weren't recognized as official parties and didn't get the research funds.

Quorum in the House
How many MPs constitute a quorum in the House of Commons?
Would you believe 20 members out of 295? The Constitution Act of 1867 and Standing Orders provide "fixed quorum of at least 20 members, including the Speaker, to constitute a meeting of the House to exercise its powers."

Paid to run
Are MPs paid while running for election?
Yes, members of the last Parliament are paid up to election day.

Even though Parliament is dissolved, government remains. The cabinet still functions, ministers are responsible for their portfolios and MPs for their constituencies.

Payday on Parliament Hill falls three days before the end of month. For example, since 30 days hath September, MPs are paid on the 27th. That's assuming it's a weekday.

At the time of the 1963 election year, MPs were grossing $64,400 a year, plus a $21,300 tax-free allowance.

The sessional allowance (pay) period for successful candidates to the next Parliament begins on the day they're elected, the House of Commons comptroller's office said.

High commissions
Why do Canada and Britain exchange high commissions, not embassies?

Ambassadors are accredited from one head of state to another. All Commonwealth countries acknowledge the Queen as its head of state, so they call their embassies in one another's capitals high commissions. Besides, the Queen is the head of state of Britain and of Canada.

Though some countries, such as India and Trinidad and Tobago became republics with presidential heads of state, they remain members of the Commonwealth.

The only difference is the name. Canada, which began the practice in 1880, hasn't considered changing it.

Canadian missions abroad
How many embassies does Canada have around the world and how many people are employed?

At last check at the beginning of 1996, Canada had 136 missions abroad, including 68 embassies; 21 high commissions; 16 consulates-general; 12 consulates (smaller missions headed by consuls, rather than consuls-general), and eight permanent missions, such as to the United Nations, the European Community and NATO.

Add four offices of Canadian embassies, which report to the

nearest ambassador; five development assistance offices; a commission and a high commission liaison office.

Canadians stationed at missions abroad at the beginning of 1996 numbered about 1,690, mostly from Foreign Affairs and International Trade but also included representatives from other government departments, such as national defence and health.

Canada also had 69 honorary consuls abroad, but foreign affairs likes to have Canadians in the posts if possible.

The number of missions have increased since 1993, when a Conservative government was in power. Missions then included 59 embassies, 21 high commissions, 18 consulates-general, five consulates, and nine permanent missions.

About 4,600 Canadian-based employees were posted at home and abroad with Foreign Affairs and International Trade. About two-thirds of them were rotational, meaning they may draw assignments at home or abroad.

Local staff employed in other countries totalled about 4,800 people.

White and green papers
What is a government white paper?

It originated in Britain as a term for a government report or policy statement to Parliament not thick enough to warrant protective covers.

In Canada, a white paper is an official document presented by a minister of the crown to state government policy on an issue. They come with covers in just about any color.

The first white paper in Canada was introduced in 1939 by finance minister Charles Dunning as an appendix to the budget. "To this day, the budget papers are often referred to as an economic white paper," researchers in the Library of Parliament wrote.

Do not confuse a white paper with a green paper. A green paper is issued by a government minister to invite public comment and discussion on an issue before a policy is formulated.

Green papers were introduced in the British Parliament in 1967.

They're bound in green covers, with the generic name Green Paper in the title. No mistaking British green papers.

Not in Canada, though. "In Canada, green covers are not used consistently so the color of the cover cannot be used as a guide," the library researchers said. Nor does Green Paper always appear in the title.

So a government "orange paper" on industrial strategy or a "purple paper" on economic policy are really green papers. Or white papers. In Ottawa, you can't tell a paper by its cover.

Tory vs *Grit*
How did Conservatives become Tories and Liberals Grits?
Tories and Grits came first. They became Conservatives and Liberals in the 19th century.

Tory was an insult, meaning outlaw, hurled at the English faction supporting the succession of Roman Catholic James II to the throne in the late 1600s. Their opponents were called Whigs, meaning horse thieves.

Over the next century, Tories came to embody the interests of the gentry and merchant classes and Whigs to represent reformers. In the 1800s, Tory leaders were described as holding conservative views and Whigs were seen as liberals. By mid-century these terms were adopted as the party names in England. Tory and Whig became nicknames.

Tory successfully crossed the ocean to Canada. Whig did not. In its place here in the mid-1800s was the term Grit, meaning pluck or an abrasive. This originated with Upper Canada reformers, who were described as "Clear grit — all sand and no dirt." Grits stuck after they and their Lower Canada allies established the Liberal party in the 1870s.

Popular vote
What is the popular vote in an election?
It's the total of all ballots cast by the electorate.

Speaker's official farm
Does the Speaker of the House of Commons get a rent-free home?

Yes. The 1.74-hectare (four-acre) "Speaker's Farm," with its 11-room heritage house and five outbuildings in Gatineau Park east of Ottawa, is one of the seven official residences of Canada. Official residences come rent-free with the trappings and responsibilities of high office.

The other six are Rideau Hall in Ottawa and The Citadel in Quebec City, residences of the governor general; 24 Sussex Drive and the summer lodge at Harrington Lake, provided for the Prime Minister; Stornoway, for the Leader of the Official Opposition; and Rideau Gate, Canada's home-away-from-home for visiting heads of state and other international VIPs.

The Farm is part of the huge Kingsmere estate in the Gatineaus bequeathed to the nation by former prime minister William Lyon Mackenzie King. The politically astute, privately eccentric King conducted much of the nation's business at the Farm during the last 15 years of his life. He died there in 1950.

The non-partisan Speaker, who presides over the House of Commons, is one of the most important figures in a parliamentary system. Other duties include overseeing House of Commons operations, its 1,500 employees and $240 million budget. The Speaker represents the House and is its host.

Speakers started renting the Farm as a summer place in 1954. The price then: $350 a year. Parliament amended the Official Residences Act in 1971, designating the Farm for the holder of the office of Speaker of the House of Commons.

Throne for the people
The Speaker's chair in the House of Commons is magnificent. How old is it? Who carved it? What kind of wood is it?

The towering chair, a symbol of the people's authority, is a replica of the Speaker's chair in the British House of Commons.

It was a gift of the United Kingdom branch of the Empire Parliamentary Association in May 1921, to replace one lost in the disastrous fire of 1916.

The Royal Arms on the canopy of the four-metre (13½-foot) chair are carved in oak taken from a section of roof erected in 1397 at Westminster Palace.

The oaken chair's scroll work and intricate carvings were copied exactly from the chair in the British Commons by Messrs. Harry Hems and Sons of Exeter, supervised by Sir Frank Baines of the Office of Works. The seat has since been made adjustable for a Speaker of any height.

Before the 1916 fire, chairs were made for each new Speaker on taking office. "The tradition was when the Speaker left the House, he took the chair with him," said Stephen Delroy, curator for the House of Commons.

"We've been trying to track them down," he said. "We know where most of them are. If people want to, they can donate them back to the House."

The Speaker's chair, from which ours was copied, was erected in the present British Parliament in 1844. It replaced a chair, believed designed by Christopher Wren, that mysteriously disappeared during a fire that destroyed most of Westminster Palace in 1834.

From 1547, the British Commons had met in the palace's St. Stephen's Chapel. The original chair displaced the chapel's altar. To this day, in Britain and in Canada, members of Parliament bow to the Speaker's chair as a sign of reverence to that altar.

Jailed MP
When was the last time a federal politician went to jail?

May 1989. Richard Grise, former chairman of the Conservatives' Quebec caucus, pleaded guilty to fraud and breach of trust, resigned his seat and spent one day behind bars.

Incidentally, we can't find a list of parliamentary jailbirds going back to Confederation. We tried the Library of Parliament, Senate

Information Centre, Speaker's Office, Public Information Office and National Archives. They don't think anyone has kept count. Odd.

Canadian, U.S. senates

How many senators are there in the Canadian Senate? How many in the American Senate?

Canada's Upper House normally has 104 senators. They're appointed by the governor general on the advice of the prime minister to serve until age 75.

The U.S. Senate has 100 senators. They're elected to six-year terms, with one-third of the seats up for grabs every two years. Each state, regardless of population, is represented by two senators.

Canada's four major regions ("divisions") have equal representation: 24 from the Maritimes (New Brunswick ten, Nova Scotia ten, Prince Edward Island four); 24 from Ontario; 24 from Quebec; 24 from the western provinces (six each from Manitoba, Saskatchewan, Alberta and British Columbia); plus six from Newfoundland and one each from the Northwest Territories and Yukon Territory.

Eight additional senators were appointed in 1989 when then prime minister Brian Mulroney moved to open passage in the Senate for the goods and services tax. This was under a constitutional provision, never before used, which allowed the appointments to break a deadlock between the Commons and Senate.

With deaths and retirements, the number of senators dropped below 104. New appointments restored the historical complement.

MPPs vs MLAs

What is the correct abbreviation designating members of a provincial legislature, MPPs or MLAs?

The designation differs according to province.

In Ontario, Members of the Provincial Parliament use the initials MPP. The Ontario Legislative Assembly officially adopted the titular distinction in 1938. The designation had been in use since before

Confederation, despite arguments it should properly be Member of the Legislative Assembly, MLA.

Quebec has the designation Member of the National Assembly, MNA, but it used to be Member of the Provincial Parliament.

Newfoundland's designation is Member of the House of Assembly, MHA.

The other seven provinces have legislative assemblies, and the members are MLAs. That's also the designation in the Yukon and Northwest Territories.

Debate over Ontario's (and formerly Quebec's) use of the designation MPP has been continuing, on and off, since 1867. Federal officials argue the British North America Act stipulates: "There shall be one Parliament for Canada."

Provincial officials counter that the legislatures are independent of the federal Parliament, enjoy the same privileges and immunities and are equal in importance so they are entitled to refer to themselves as "parliaments."

The arguments seem to have less to do with semantics than with the relative powers of the two levels of government.

Persons at last
Which province was first to give women the right to vote?
Quebec women of property could vote in municipal elections in 1809, four decades before their sisters anywhere else in Canada. They were among the first women in the world to have the vote. But this right was taken away in 1849 and not fully restored until almost a century later.

Ontario women who owned property were allowed to vote for school trustees in 1850 and by 1900 women had gained the right to vote in school and municipal elections in all provinces except Quebec.

While the women's suffrage movement was strongest in central Canada, the Western provinces were first to acknowledge the role of women in building their societies. Manitoba, Saskatchewan and Alberta granted provincial equality in 1916. British Columbia and

Ontario followed the next year. Women were allowed to vote provincially in Nova Scotia in 1918, New Brunswick in 1919, Prince Edward Island in 1922. Newfoundland, which joined Canada in 1949, had given women the franchise in 1925.

Federally, women in the armed forces or those with relatives in the armed forces were given the right to vote by the Wartime Elections Act of 1917. On Victoria Day, 1918, all Canadian women from age 21 could vote in federal elections, including Quebecoise, who'd be denied the provincial vote for another 22 years.

In 1919, women gained the right to seek election to the House of Commons. But this was not full political equality. They still couldn't sit in the Senate.

The Supreme Court of Canada in the famous "Person's Case" blocked the appointment of women to the Senate ruling in 1928 that under the British North America Act of 1867, "Women are persons in matters of pain and suffering, but not matters of rights or privileges."

This ruling, against Henrietta Muir and her Alberta suffragettes, was reversed the following year in an appeal to the British Privy Council, which found in the Supreme Court decision "a relic of days more barbarous than ours."

The last barbarous relic was destroyed April 25, 1940, when Quebec women, led by Thérése Casgrain, at last won the right to vote in provincial elections.

12

—

STANDING ON GUARD

Strength in numbers
How many people are there in a squad, platoon, company, battalion, regiment, brigade, division and corps?
A lot depends on the tasks assigned various units, say officers at the Department of National Defence in Ottawa. But, basically, a squad is six people, a platoon about 36 people and an infantry company about 120. Three or four companies make up an infantry battalion, with three battalions per infantry regiment.

A tank regiment, however, is made up of four armored squadrons and a headquarters squadron. The armored squadrons would each have 19 tanks and about 100 people, but a headquarters squadron has a larger number of people to carry out its functions.

Numbers of planes and personnel in an air force squadron also vary depending on their mission. A Canadian Forces fighter squadron usually has 12 to 18 CF-18 aircraft, but 24 fighters were assigned the squadron based in Qatar during the Gulf War.

Size of an infantry brigade depends on the various mixes of equipment — infantry, armor, artillery, engineers, tactical aviation, field ambulances and logistical units — but generally it's about 5,000 people. In the Canadian Forces, they're called "brigade groups" because they have their own support elements.

In other countries with larger armies, these are usually attached at the division level.

Three brigades would make up a division, with about three divisions to a corps. An army is made up of any number of corps.

Canadians in foreign armies

Are there any restrictions on Canadian citizens serving in a foreign army?

Canadian citizens are not prohibited from serving in another country's armed forces. And if the foreign country requires you to become a citizen to serve in its military, you could keep your Canadian citizenship.

But if that country's requirements does not allow dual citizenship and you must renounce your Canadian citizenship to serve in its military and you chose to formally do so, you'd no longer be Canadian.

You would not be allowed to come back as a Canadian. You'd have to apply for landed immigrant status.

In the U.S., a Pentagon official said Army Regulation 135-100 states that an alien accepted into the military must apply to become a permanent resident. To remain in the military for more than eight years, the person must obtain U.S. citizenship. Canadians can have dual citizenship in the U.S.

Landed immigrants in Canada who wish to serve in another country's armed forces should check with the immigration department.

Though there doesn't seem to be anything in the Canada Immigration Act to prevent landed immigrants from going back because they're feeling patriotic or to fulfil an obligation, those absent from Canada without a good excuse for more than 183 days in a year are liable to lose landed immigrant status.

In general, landed immigrants who expect to be away for more than six months are required to obtain a returning resident's permit or may be deemed to have abandoned Canada.

Of course, all this is in a peacetime context. A Canadian con-victed of going over to the enemy in wartime could face a series of penalties under the War Measures Act, and up to capital punish-ment under the National Defence Act.

Military numerals
How do they come up with the numbers to designate military units, such as the Royal 22nd Regiment, etc.?

Every country has its own system. Ours is derived from the British and to some extent the French military systems, says historian Steve Harris at the Department of National Defence's History Directorate in Ottawa.

"The British system of numbering units is based on seniority. For example, the First Regiment of Foot was first formed after the restoration of Charles II. The Second Regiment was the second one formed and so on.

"It was the same thing with our old militia. The First Regiment was formed in Montreal. The Second was the Queen's Own Rifles in Toronto, the Third was the Victoria Rifles in Montreal."

But there are aberrations. From time to time, units disappeared, written out of militia lists and leaving a vacancy. When a new mili-tia unit formed in another locality, the vacant number would be backfilled, he says. Another anomaly that became the rule occurred in World War I. Canada did not use existing militia units as the basis for the overseas expeditionary force and new composite battalions were formed.

For instance, the new Toronto Regiment (3rd Battalion) was formed with members of militia regiments, but not the regiments themselves, Harris said.

Another example: the 22nd Regiment of militia was located in Woodstock, but the Royal 22nd Regiment (Van Doos) in Montreal had no connection with it. The Van Doos were formed as the 22nd Battalion of the Canadian Expeditionary Force. When World War I was over, these outfits simply kept their own numbers.

By 1914, we had virtually done away with numerical designations for militia regiments anyway, so there was no confusion over having two 22nd regiments. They were known by their names, Harris said.

Rambo — Canadian-style
Does the Canadian military have elite units similar to the British SAS or American Rangers?

This is one of those yes and no answers. "We have similar, over-lapping functions, capabilities and duties, but you can't make a direct comparison," said Major Laz Tollas, at the Department of National Defence Headquarters in Ottawa.

What we have is a Special Service Force (SSF) based in Petawawa, Ont., made up of airborne commando groups, headquarters, engineers, service support, artillery groups, and an aviation component. The special service is capable of carrying out long-range reconnaissance or raids by stealth, similar to the kinds of tasks carried out by the British Special Air Services and Special Boat Services, the American Navy Seals or the U.S. Army's Green Berets or Rangers.

While not specializing in anti-terrorist activities, such as the SAS, the Canadian SSF is capable of carrying out some of this kind of work, said Tollas, who served four years in commando groups.

Airborne commandos, since the disbanding of the scandal prone Airborne Regiment, are recruited from parachute companies attached to infantry regiments, such as the Princess Pats, Royal Canadian Regiment and Van Doos. Much of the commando training focuses on carrying out special tasks within Canada.

An example: if Government X (or a heavily-armed drug gang) violated the nation's sovereignty in setting up a base in a remote, impenetrable area, the Special Service Force gets the call to solve the problem.

Hostage rescue in anti-terrorist actions on Canadian soil used to be the responsibility of the Royal Canadian Mounted Police Special Response Team, though military commando units could be called to assist.

But in April 1993, the federal government assigned Canadian Forces to take over from the RCMP the role of hostage rescuers in anti-terrorist action, and a new elite unit was formed, Joint Task Force 2.

Officers at DND headquarters declined to discuss the unit, its make-up, capabilities, equipment, training or other aspects of the outfit designated for this role. Major Rick Jones, the officer authorized to speak to the press about it, described it only as "a highly trained unit in the geographical area of Ottawa."

Obviously, Joint Task Force 2 is highly classified. Presumably, from what is known of similar units in other countries, members would be chosen for their character, discipline, skills, initiative and ability to work in teams. They would be rehearsed in rescuing hostages from planes, trains, buses and other vehicles, and from buildings. They'd study successes and failures in hostage rescues, by foreign anti-terrorism teams. Negotiators would be on the team.

Though they may have some training abroad, they would operate in Canada. Overseas, if one of our embassies or airliners was seized, the Canadian Security Intelligence Service (operating behind the scenes, of course) would provide that country's anti-terrorist service with information and advice to help resolve the matter.

Our last V.C. winner
Who was the last Canadian to win the Victoria Cross?

Robert Hampton Gray, 27, of Nelson, B.C., a Royal Canadian Navy lieutenant attached to the British Pacific fleet. On August 9, 1945 — only five days before World War II ended — he led a group of Corsair fighters attacking targets on Japan's east coast.

Flak set Gray's plane afire. He might have dropped his bombs at random and ditched in an enemy bay, but he chose to keep diving on an anchored destroyer.

He was less than 20 metres (22 yards) away when he dropped his load, sinking the destroyer. A second later his blazing fighter sank beside it. Gray was killed.

Incidentally, that was the day the U.S. dropped its second atomic bomb and forced Japan to surrender.

A total of 93 Canadians have won the Victoria Cross. It was instituted in 1856 by Queen Victoria. The first Canadian winner was Alexander Roberts (1833-1868) of Toronto, a lieutenant in the 11th Hussars, for heroism in rescuing his sergeant under enemy guns during the charge of the Light Brigade at Balaklava in the Crimean War. He died in a hunting accident in Abyssinia in 1868.

Death by firing squad
What can you tell me about firing squads? Are there five people on a firing squad, only one with a bullet in his gun?

Although it's popularly supposed that the death penalty has been abolished in Canada, capital punishment remains on the books under the National Defence Act for 32 offences involving cowardice, desertion, unlawful surrender and treachery, spying for the enemy and for mutiny accompanied by violence.

Theoretically, a formal firing squad — though the method of execution is not specifically defined in the act — could be mustered, even in peacetime. Records show the normal complement in a Canadian military firing squad was ten soldiers commanded by an officer. In a few instances, squads were made up of more than ten men or as few as seven. They usually came from the accused's unit.

Each member was issued a live round for his rifle. Later, with the squad absent, a blank shell replaced the bullet in one of the weapons. None of them knew who drew the blank, "but they all might believe they might have the blank," said historian Harris of DND's directorate of history.

The last Canadian soldier was executed by firing squad on July 5, 1945, "for crimes committed in Rome of murder." He'd been found guilty after a general court martial in Italy.

The number of Canadian soldiers shot by firing squads or British or French soldiers serving on Canadian soil over the centuries has not been documented. But *Shot at Dawn*, a book by Julian Putkowski and Julian Sykes, published in Britain in 1989, says 25 soldiers from Canadian regiments were shot by British firing squads in World War I.

Desertion, cowardice, falling asleep on duty and striking an officer led to court martials and executions, they reported.

The punishment in many cases appeared to be particularly grotesque in relation to the charges. In one example, a private was executed because he went missing from his battalion for seven hours.

Directions to Flanders' fields
Where is "Flanders' field," the field mentioned in the poem?

Flanders, an ancient Flemish principality, extends along the English Channel from just below Dunkirk in France to Antwerp in Belgium and southern Zeeland province in Holland, then down to run along the French and Belgian border.

It was during the Second Battle of Ypres in 1915 that the Canadian poet-soldier and physician Lieutenant-Colonel John McCrae wrote *In Flanders' Fields*. This is the story behind the poem, pieced together from his letters home to Guelph:

The medical officer of the 1st Artillery Brigade was in the back of a field ambulance rattling along near the Yser canal. It was early May and scarlet poppies covered the shell-pocked landscape. A flight of birds wheeled in the distance. About 100 metres north of the Ypres bridge, the ambulance passed wooden crosses marking the graves of Canadian, British, French, Belgian and Moroccan soldiers.

One marked the grave of his friend, Lieutenant Alex Helmer of Ottawa. Helmer died of shrapnel wounds May 2 as stretcher bearers carried him to McCrae's field station. McCrae had set his cross in the ground.

In the ambulance, McCrae placed a dispatch pad on his knee and wrote:

In Flanders' fields the poppies grow
Between the crosses, row on row

That mark our place; and in the sky
The larks, still bravely singing, fly
Scarce heard amid the guns below.

He wrote three verses. He finished the poem in 20 minutes. These lines taken from McCrae's manuscript in the Osler Library, Montreal, show the first line ending "poppies grow," but lines in handwritten versions to family members are said to read "poppies blow."

McCrae died of pneumonia on January 28, 1918, age 45. He was buried in the Wimereux cemetery, near Boulogne, France, a soldier's grave like the ones in the fields of Flanders.

No draft in Canada

If Canada goes to war, would the draft be imposed?

"Essentially, there is no draft in Canada," defence officials will assure you. There'd have to be an Act of Parliament to bring one in.

Even during World Wars I and II, long and divisive deliberations over conscription preceded the enactment of the draft. The first preference was to take volunteers. Nobody in government brought up the idea of a draft during the Mideast crisis that culminated in the Gulf War in early 1991.

During the Iraq-Kuwait crisis, External Affairs Minister Joe Clark told University of Western Ontario students: "I know of nobody who is contemplating conscription in this country for anybody under any circumstances."

Elections were fought in 1917 and 1942 over conscription and, though eventually enacted, only 24,132 conscripts arrived in France before World War I ended and only 12,908 went overseas in World War II.

But rather than belligerents or meddlers in conflicts around the world, Canada maintains a proud role as mediator and peacekeeper.

13

MONEY AND OTHER VALUABLES

Phoney as a $3 bill, eh?
When was the $3 bill last issued in Canada? Whose portrait was on it?

The last $3 bank note, dated 1886, was issued by the St. Stephen's Bank of New Brunswick. Queen Victoria's portrait graced the note.

The $3 bill was actually prohibited by the Bank Act of 1871, but the ban didn't apply to the St. Stephen's Bank in St. Stephen, N.B. — which wasn't listed on a schedule of banks attached to the act — and it continued to issue them, said Graham Esler, chief curator of the Bank of Canada's Currency Museum.

Esler wasn't sure how many were issued "but some are out there. It's a very scarce note." And much, much more valuable to collectors than the $3 face value, redeemable at an agency of the Bank of Canada.

An earlier $3 note was issued by the Colonial Bank, which failed in 1859.

"It goes back so far that most people just don't know that ($3 bills) existed," Esler said. "Most people don't know the $4 note existed either, or the $6, $7 and $8 notes."

While neither the Dominion of Canada, nor the Province of

Canada before it, nor the Bank of Canada ever issued $3 notes, the government printed $4 bills up to 1911. They were replaced with $5 bills the following year.

"They look kind of strange to us now, but $4 was the equivalent of one pound sterling. So when we had an $8 bill, that was worth two pounds sterling. That was the relationship," Esler said.

Bogus leaf on penny
What are the leaves shown on the Canadian one-cent piece? They aren't maple leaves.

Now that you mention it, something does look odd. Esler explained why: "They're a bastardized form of a sugar maple leaf. Artistic licence has been taken."

The coin was designed in 1937 by George Kruger-Gray — that's his KG on it — who also designed the Canadian nickel. "He wasn't really setting out to be botanically correct. He was simply choosing a symbol that had been associated with Canada almost from the beginning," Esler said.

Jane Young, a lecturer on leaf identification at the U of T's faculty of forestry, pointed out: "Maple trees have opposite leaf arrangement — opposite side of the twig. This (one-cent piece) seems to show an alternate leaf arrangement."

Canada's neglected coin
Whatever happened to the old 50-cent coin?

Nothing, and that's the trouble. Canadians don't bother using it and coin slots don't recognize it. Aside from collectors, there's little demand for the coin that's been around since 1870.

Currently, the circulation coin shows Queen Elizabeth in profile wearing a jewelled diadem and on the reverse is the Canadian coat of arms and motto. The diameter is 29.72 mm. "It's produced to order in our Winnipeg plant," said Barbara Steele of the Royal Canadian Mint. "But in terms of everyday circulation, it's not a coin that's required."

The mint produces coins according to demand. Criteria include numbers used in transactions and requested by banks.

Collectors did send production of the 50-cent coins to 987,000 in 1994, but that was fewer than one in 1,000 of the 1,075,539,000 coins minted. Only 393,000 were produced in 1993 and a mere 248,000 in 1992.

The lowest mintage came during the Great Depression in 1932, when only 19,213 pieces were produced. The greatest number of them ever struck was 12,629,974 in 1965.

The $1,000 question
I saw a commercial featuring a $10,000 bill on television. But what is the largest paper denomination in Canada?
The largest denomination note in Canada is $1,000, note the folks at the Bank of Canada. Its dominant color is rose, Queen Elizabeth is on the face and the scene on the other side is of Anse St. Jean on the Saguenuay River. The note has been in circulation since 1954.

The largest denomination note ever in this country was a $50,000 bill. But it was never in public circulation. The "Bank legal" was only used to transfer funds between banks, from 1918 to 1934. The old $50,000 note is a highlight of the currency museum in the Bank of Canada's headquarters on Sparks Street in Ottawa.

The Bank of England had notes for 1 million pounds sterling up to about two centuries ago for internal accounting.

The highest denomination note ever in general circulation in the U.S. was a $10,000 bill, printed until 1944. The largest bank note issued in the U.S. today is $100.

Cash in Canada
How much money is printed in Canada in a year?
You have to distinguish between notes that are printed and notes put into circulation. Worn notes are continually being taken out of circulation and new notes put in.

The best way of looking at this is to examine what happened to notes in circulation. The Bank of Canada keeps close tabs on notes in circulation, notes printed, returned, destroyed, or in storage.

The average in a typical month in the mid-1990s was 1.176 billion notes in circulation with a total value of $26.9 billion, said Garret Bilkes, assistant chief of systems research in the office of banking operations.

A breakdown in individual denominations for that month shows $163 million in $1 bills out there six years after being replaced by the loonie. Other denominations (in round numbers) $454 million in $2 notes, $690 million in $5s, $940 million in $10s, $7.32 billion in $20s, $3.65 billion in $50s, $11.2 billion in $100s and $2.2 billion in $1,000s.

Somewhere, probably in the hands of collectors, are an extra $23,000 or so in $500 notes and about $46,000 in $25 bills — denominations unissued since early this century — plus almost $8 million in banknotes issued in the 19th century by chartered banks, provinces and the Dominion of Canada.

Total number of coins in circulation is unknown, but the Royal Canadian Mint has struck more than 18 billion circulation coins since 1976 alone. The government has been minting coins in Canada since 1858. But once issued, they don't come back, unless damaged.

In round numbers, the number of coins struck with the date 1994 were: 47 million loonies, 1 million 50-cent pieces, 94 million quarters, 139 million dimes, 99 million nickels and 696 million pennies. Add 'em up.

About 300 million $2 coins were to be issued in the 18 months following their launch on February 19, 1996.

Goodbye, bill
When did they stop printing $1 bills?

The Bank of Canada issued the last $1 bill on June 30, 1989. They have gradually been taken out of circulation by the commercial bank network, returned to the Bank of Canada and destroyed.

They're legal tender and some are still around, but the central bank no longer issues souvenir sheets. If you'd like one, look up a collector or an acquaintance who might part with a keepsake.

The $1 coin, nicknamed the loonie, was introduced two years before the last $1 banknote rolled off the presses. Initially, a lot of people disliked the loonie — $1 bills were easier and lighter to carry and didn't roll under the couch.

Two pieces of eight
Where did the expression "two bits" for 25 cents originate?
English colonies in North America weren't allowed to mint coins. So foreign coins were used to increase supply, including Spanish dollars — pieces of eight. These silver pesos could be cut into eight bits to make change. Two bits were a quarter dollar and four bits were a half dollar.

Size of a thin dime
Why is the size of a dime smaller than a nickel?
That stems from the time they used to be made of silver. If the dime was bigger, the silver content would have been worth more than its face value of ten cents.

The silver dime appeared in 1858 when the Province of Canada adopted the decimal system based on the dollar. The Victoria ten-cent piece, minted between 1870 and 1901, was .925 silver and .075 copper.

Until 1922, when its composition was changed to nickel, the Canadian five-cent coin was also silver but was smaller than the dime. That year, the diameter was increased to 21.21 millimetres, similar in size to the U.S. nickel, which was in plentiful supply in Canada. The dime retained its size and silver content.

But silver in the dime was gradually reduced over the years as the price of the precious metal rose. Finally, speculators sent silver prices soaring in the late 1960s.

The Royal Canadian Mint struck its last silver ten-cent pieces for circulation in early 1968. Its composition was .500 fine silver and

.500 copper. Production couldn't keep up with demand because the coins were hoarded by the speculators.

New ten-cent coins made of nickel were authorized for minting in August, 1968. The dime has been made of nickel ever since, said Diane Plouffe Reardon, who fielded the question for the mint.

But the dime's traditional size wasn't changed. People were used to it, it was similar in size to the U.S. dime, and dime slots across the country — for everything from pay phones to parking meters to candy machines — wouldn't have to be changed. The costs would have been astronomical.

Banks printed dollars
Where does the word dollar come from?

It originates from the German word *thaler* (*thal*, meaning dale or valley), adopted from the *Joachimsthaler*, a coin minted in Bohemia's St. Joachim Valley in 1519. Spelling changed over the centuries, and *thaler* also became *daler* and *dalar*. The Germans replaced it as the monetary unit with the Deutsche Mark in 1873.

The dollar, equal to 100 cents, became the U.S. monetary unit in 1792. Canada officially adopted the dollar and monetary decimal system in 1858. Our first government-printed paper dollars appeared in 1870.

Paper dollars in circulation before then were issued by private, commercial banks. The Bank of Montreal issued paper dollars almost immediately after it was founded in 1817. Circulation of money issued by commercial banks ceased on December 31, 1949, 15 years after the Bank of Canada was established. That was the deadline when the banks had to exchange their currency for Bank of Canada notes.

Mystery of the dollar sign
What is the origin of the dollar sign? Does it have two strokes through it to represent the two columns Samson pulled down?

The origin is obscure. One theory is the S represents a broken 8, from the old Spanish pesos known as pieces of 8 (valued at eight reals). They were also called Spanish dollars in the early days of North American settlement. Strokes appeared on Mexican pieces of eight in the early 18th century.

Another theory maintains the $ sign is an overlapping of the U and S in the initials for United States.

But evidence suggests the dollar sign probably originated from the abbreviation SP for Spanish peso, which circulated widely in the United States and in the British colonies.

Gradually, people wrote the S on top of the P and eventually used only S with two bars through it to represent the P.

The earliest dollar marks found in colonial documents were in the ledgers and correspondence of a New Orleans businessman, Oliver Pollock, from about 1775.

Pollock's initial entries show an S and a P made in a continuous line, with the P formed in a sort of double stroke of the pen, one line going down and then up to the curl of the P.

By 1778, Pollock was in the habit of scrawling his double-P strokes over the S.

Until Pollock's entries, the most usual symbols for money found in English-speaking North America were those for pounds, shillings and pence.

Pollock shipped goods to the U.S. government and among the Congressional recipients was Robert Morris, who became the first high official to use the dollar mark.

Canadians quickly picked up on the dollar sign because American currency circulated here. In 1858, Canada adopted the decimal system based on the dollar and the $ was here to stay.

We couldn't find any reference to the dollar sign and the Old Testament story of Samson's destruction of the Philistine temple.

Good ol' days, eh?
What were the wages at the turn of the century?
Pay in Canada at the turn of the century averaged about $1 a day. The 1901 census showed the average wage across the country was

$292 a year. Men averaged $334 and women $176.

The average work week was edging down to 44 hours a week.

Ads in *The Toronto Daily Star* that May showed cheese at 11 cents a pound, and coffee at 19 cents a pound. Tomatoes were 25 cents for two pounds, probably because of the cost of importing them from the U.S.

Sale prices of men's suits were $5.45 to $12. A derby hat cost 69 cents. Women's skirts were $1.29 and up. A six-room house with a bath in a working class area was advertised at $735. A far grander one in the elegant Admiral Road area was $5,000.

Isolation pay
Do federal civil servants doing similar jobs in Halifax, Montreal, Toronto, the Prairies, Vancouver and the Northwest Territories make the same salary?

Yes and no. The basic salaries are the same, depending on job classifications and agreements between the Treasury Board and 17 civil service unions. But an isolation allowance is paid, depending on remoteness of a post and other criteria.

Also, Treasury and 14 bargaining units within six of the unions — representing such jobs as hospital services, general labor and ship repairers — have negotiated regional rates of pay.

Criteria for these are whether wages in a region vary significantly from the national average, whether the pay scale is in line with that in the area's private sector and on the availability of recruits for specific trades.

A tip on taxes
Are you supposed to leave a tip in restaurants covering the total bill, which includes GST and the PST, or just the subtotal?

Don't tip on taxes. Calculate the tip on the subtotal. Look at it this way: the goods and services tax and provincial sales tax doesn't add to your enjoyment of the meal, to the quality of service, or enhance the ambience of the restaurant. Paying taxes surely detracts from the pleasure of the evening.

If it doesn't, you must be the federal minister of finance dining on an expense account.

14

TO YOUR HEALTH

Medicare vs private insurance
If I moved to the U.S., how much would medical insurance cost in order to give me the same coverage I get under medicare in Canada?

A lot depends on your age, fitness, previous health record and family medical history. But a study found the equivalent private insurance in the U.S. costs about $2,500 a year per single person, and $10,000 for a family of four in Canadian dollars.

Medicare's cost would be under $2,000 a year on average across Canada for a single person and about $7,500 for a family of four.

The figures come from data compiled by Dr. Donald Redelmeier of the University of Toronto Department of Medicine and Wellesley Hospital Research Institute, and economist Victor Fuchs, of Stanford University in California.

Results of their study "Hospital Expenditures in the U.S. and Canada" appeared in the March 18, 1993, issue of the *New England Journal of Medicine*.

In Canada, financing is done indirectly through federal and provincial taxes, whereas in the U.S., it's done directly through insurance premiums and out-of-pocket expenses, Redelmeier said.

Costs of health services are lower in this country. For example, bills for physician services in the U.S. are on average about 2½ times higher than ours, as you'll see in the next item.

Aside from lower costs, there are other advantages to the Canadian system, Redelmeier said. In the U.S., insurance companies do a lot of experience rating. "They'll ask a lot of questions on your past health, your family health, whether or not you plan to get pregnant and so on."

The coverage is individualized, meaning insurers will offer you a lower price to get you to subscribe if you're young, healthy and in good shape, he said. On the other end of the scale, if you've got a lot of medical problems, "it can become quite difficult for you to pay your medical insurance rates."

Also, individuals may find it difficult to buy coverage for themselves. "Most commonly, everybody who gets insurance, gets it through their employer," Redelmeier said. Insurance firms "are much more willing to sell to a large group.

"This is a big problem for the U.S. If you lose your job, you don't just lose your employment, you lose your health insurance."

Are U.S. doctors richer?
Are doctors in the United States really two or three times better off than Canadian doctors?
The bottom line is no, according to Redelmeier's data bank. That's despite the fact that costs for physicians' services in the U.S. are on average about 2½ times greater than similar services in Canada, his studies show. Surgical fees are more than three times as high. Counselling and evaluation services are less than twice as high.

But the actual take home pay of U.S. doctors is only about a third higher than in Canada, according to Redelmeier's study published in *The New England Journal* of Medicine (September 27, 1990).

Reasons are many. All Canadians have comprehensive health insurance. Physicians are promptly and fully paid from one source and according to a negotiated schedule of fees.

In the U.S., a physician's staff has to deal with myriad insurers, from Medicaid to company plans (and each likely offers a different level of coverage). This increases the administrative overhead.

Then U.S. physicians encounter patients without insurance of any kind who just can't pay their bills (perhaps 30 million Americans, according to U.S. advocates of a universal medicare system). Many millions of others are only partially covered and many of these patients just can't afford to make up the shortfall.

People in the U.S. lacking full medical insurance are reluctant to visit their doctors unless absolutely necessary, which can mean a simple medical problem may become a major problem.

Data shows U.S. doctors typically see fewer patients than their Canadian colleague. And to attract patients in a highly competitive profession, more money is spent on amenities, marketing and overhead.

Finally, liability insurance is crippling for doctors in the litigious United States. The average American physician is seven times more likely to be sued for malpractice than a Canadian counterpart.

On average, a Canadian physician can expect to be sued once every 50 years. In the U.S., the average doctor is sued once every seven years.

Hospital bills abroad
What is the cost of hospital stays per day in Britain, the United States, Western Europe, etc.?
The range runs from $87 a day for a hospital stay in Japan to $1,000 a day in the United States. In Canada, the cost was $408. These averages are all in 1990 U.S. dollars.

In the absence of any studies on the topic, our figures were extrapolated by a friendly number cruncher in the Health Care Financing Administration of the U.S. Department of Health and Human Services from general data supplied by member nations to the Organization for Economic Co-operation and Development.

For the United Kingdom, the nation-wide average was $202 a day; France, $233; Germany, $169.

The financing administration also calculated expenditures per stay. For the U.K. it was $2,546 (U.S.); France, $2,897, Germany, $2,666; Japan $4,279, and for the U.S., $8,761. It was $5,828 in 1989 for Canada.

The health department number cruncher explained the apparent discrepancy between low Japanese per-day costs and relatively high per-stay figures, saying chronic and nursing-home care are included with acute-care costs in Japanese data.

The average hospital stay in Japan is about 50 days, whereas in the United States, "it's in and out." Also, medical care is less intensive than in North American acute-care hospitals. In Japan, "You go into hospital for rest and relaxation and you stay."

Meanwhile, data from the Ontario Hospital Association showed the basic cost of a patient in a provincial hospital averages $360 (Canadian) a day. That's for nursing care, three meals, a hospital bed and clean sheets. It doesn't include drugs, bandages, dressings, doctors and so on.

Age and health
At age 65, what percentage of Canadian men and women will be healthy and not experiencing any major illness?
"About 73 per cent of men and women aged 65 and over have indicated that they perceive their health status to be excellent/very good to good and about 27 per cent to be in fair/poor condition," said Cyril Nair, chief for health care at Statistics Canada.

The data comes from StatsCan's 1994 National Population Health Survey. More than 5,000 seniors were surveyed in the 20,000 households studied across the country. This study didn't include seniors living in institutions.

Some aspects of the health of Canadians at age 65 and over in households: about 37 per cent of men (including 28 per cent aged 75 and over) and 28 per cent of women (including 22 per cent aged 75 and over) said they were active to moderately active in physical activity; about 72 per cent of men and 65 per cent of women reported no pain or discomfort from any of their activities; about 23 per cent of men surveyed said they did not have any chronic disease, 28 per cent mentioned one disease and 13 per cent listed four or more. Of women, 17 per cent said they had no chronic disease, 30 per cent mentioned one and 20 per cent listed four or more.

Of those reporting chronic conditions, arthritis and rheumatism were listed by 33 per cent of men and 46 per cent of women; high blood pressure by 23 per cent of men and 33 per cent of women; heart disease by 19 per cent of men and 15 per cent of women; and 17 per cent of men and 19 per cent of women had back problems.

About 17 per cent of men said they'd taken no medications in the previous month and 27 per cent said they'd had one or two. For women, 12 per cent hadn't needed medication and 50 per cent had one or two medications.

But of those taking medication, 55 per cent of men and 61 per cent of women said they'd used pain relievers in the previous month. About 46 per cent of men had blood pressure medication or heart medication. About 55 per cent of women had blood pressure or heart medications.

As for functional limitations, about 82 per cent of men and 87 per cent of women mentioned vision. Cognitive limitations (such as memory loss) were reported by about 37 per cent of both sexes and chronic pain by 27 per cent of men and 34 per cent of women.

The mean number of contacts with doctors was six times in the previous year for both men and women and 17 per cent had a stay in hospital.

According to 1991 tables, the average life expectancy at birth was about 75 years for males and 81 years for females. But for men who've attained the age of 65, it's about 81 years. For women, it's about 85 years.

For men who'd attained the age of 80, it's about 87 years and women at 80 have a life expectancy of 89½ years.

Ripe old age
How many people in Canada are 100 years old or more?
About 3,700 and rising quickly, according to the 1991 census. Another 1,200 were expected to become centurians that year. With people living longer, healthier lives, the number is expected to double by 2011 and reach 25,000 by 2046 when Baby Boomers start turning 100.

A total of 93,840 people counted during the 1991 census were aged 90 and more.

About 1,000 people a year reach the century mark, based on the number of birthday greetings the Governor General sends out annually to centenarians. Greetings went to 1,186 people celebrating their 100th birthday or more in 1993. The numbers were 1,347 people in 1992, 1,149 in 1991, and 1,082 in 1990.

The messages are sent only at five-year intervals, and on request, though they may be issued every year for 105th birthdays and over.

Meanwhile, of the 93,840 people 90 years or more during the census, 68,790 were women and 25,050 were men.

The great flu epidemic of 1918
I was born in March 1918. When did the great flu epidemic hit Toronto? I'm told my oldest brother saved my life, as all the rest of the family was down with the flu.
"The epidemic struck the city almost like a cyclone, assuming epidemic proportions on or about October 9th, and continued until November 2nd, when it subsided quite as rapidly as it began," Dr. Charles Hastings, Toronto's medical officer of health reported on November 18, 1918. "Toronto with a population of 490,000 had 1,614 deaths" in that span.

But *Toronto Star* files show deaths from influenza or complications, particularly pneumonia (penicillin wasn't discovered till 1928), continued through November and December, with five deaths recorded as late as Christmas week that year.

More than 60 per cent of the 1,614 victims at the height of the epidemic were aged 20 to 50, Hasting said in his report, found in the Toronto City Archives. A total of 455 people were 20 to 29 years old.

But the death rate in Toronto was less than in other cities, and Hastings credited public awareness, preparation and the work of health professionals. Boston, with a population just under 800,000, recorded more than 4,000 deaths by October 19. Montreal, a city of 640,000 people, counted 3,892 deaths. Buffalo, with 476,000 people, had 2,170 deaths.

The virus, carried by troops returning from Europe, worked its way across Canada from September to the end of December. The national death toll stood at more than 50,000, *Star* files show. One in six persons suffered from the flu. Churches and theaters closed for weeks and meetings were cancelled in October, when the epidemic was at its peak. Prairie farmers wore gauze masks in the fields. Villages in outlying areas of Quebec and Labrador, the hardest hit areas, were wiped out.

The epidemic of "Spanish Influenza," named from its heavy toll in Spain including the death of King Alfonso XIII, left about 21 million people dead world-wide that spring, summer and fall.

Sports and medicare

Do professional American athletes playing for teams in Canada get Canadian medicare coverage?

Yes. Like migrant farm help, accident-prone millionaires are eligible for medicare if they have "employment authorization" from Employment and Immigration Canada. Their teams arrange it. The players merely state their intention to stay in Canada at least three months.

Doctors and their families

Is it really true that medical doctors are not allowed to treat their immediate families? Why not?

The Code of Ethics of the Canadian Medical Association states that physicians may provide only minor or emergency services for their immediate families or themselves.

From time to time, notices are issued reminding doctors of the importance of this section of the code, under patient care.

A 1988 notice from the Ontario College of Physicians and Surgeons, for example, warned: "Serious problems arise when physicians become primary providers of medical care to themselves or to members of their immediate family. The objectivity necessary to render reasonable care and limit self-indulgent and potentially harmful treatment is lost by most practitioners in this situation."

It said an increasing number of physicians were finding themselves in trouble by ignoring these principles, particularly in relation to narcotics and controlled drug prescriptions, such as painkillers and barbituates.

For example, if a physician's spouse or children were in a great deal of pain, the physician might be inclined to provide painkillers as they demand them, which might not be in the best medical interests of the patient.

A physician treating himself or a family member would be liable to charges of professional misconduct before the college's discipline committee. If narcotics or controlled drugs were involved, the federal Minister of Health, under the Narcotics Control Act, could revoke the physician's privilege to prescribe, possess or dispense them.

When doctors get sick

Why don't doctors ever seem to get sick? Why don't they pick up the bugs going around?

They do. But while doctors meet a lot of people with colds, flu and other illnesses — so do we — they probably get sick less often and are less sick than the rest of us. Their insurance statistics indicate that.

"The reason is they're probably in contact with all the germs. Their immunity level is very high. Their natural immunity is stimulated," said Ted Bodway, director of health policy for the Ontario Medical Association.

Even when they've picked up a virus, you'll find them at work, probably examining you for the same bug, looking down your throat and telling you to say "ah."

"Doctors know there's not much use isolating themselves when they have the flu. That's because the three days before they felt unwell," and Bodway stressed the before, "are the most contagious days of the illness. By the time you feel sick, you're less contagious than the day before you felt sick. "So there's not much use in trying to avoid the public. You'd have to avoid the public all the time."

Also, while a doctor is home in bed, the office overhead (rent, staff salaries, etc.) continues to ring up. "Our statistics — we run the insurance program for doctors — show that doctors are just bears to go back to work. They go back quicker than just about anybody else."

When doctors die

What happens to a doctor's records after he or she dies? For example, what happens if a patient's offspring need genetic information, such as on a hereditary disease?

Presumably, you're talking about your own medical records. You'd have to obtain them from the deceased doctor's estate. Perhaps the records were transferred to another doctor who took over the practice.

If they're a parent's records, the parent would have to obtain them. If the parent is also deceased, offspring may never have access to them, unless they can persuade a court to allow it. Health information is confidential, a matter between doctor and patient.

Also, there's no law or directive that specifically forbids a dead doctor's survivors or estate from immediately destroying patient records, checks of the Ontario College of Physicians and Surgeons, the Ontario Medical Association and health ministry show.

"There's no prohibition against it. It's just not done, as a matter of course. They could be liable," said James Maclean, director of public affairs for the college.

He cited a case in which the Supreme Court of Canada ruled that the relationship between a doctor and a patient is a fiduciary one. All information about the patient given the doctor — including information from specialists — should be made available to the patient, it ruled.

"It would seem to me that since the patient has the right to see the records and have a copy of the record while the doctor is alive, that would also apply when the doctor dies," Maclean said.

But the issue is far from clear. The Health Disciplines Act says patient records must be maintained by physicians for a period of six years from the date of the last entry, or until the doctor ceases to be engaged in the practice of medicine, whichever occurs first. The Regulated Health Professions Act, which will replace it, has similar wording.

Barbara Selkirk of the Ontario health ministry said the custom has been that patient records are held for at least a year by deceased doctors' estates before they're destroyed.

15

A FEW WORDS IN PASSING

Allo, Anglo

What is an allophone, mentioned in all these commentaries after the Quebec referendum? The dictionary definition makes no sense.

"Allophone" was adapted in Canada during unity debates of the 1970s and '80s to mean a resident of Quebec whose mother tongue is neither French nor English. Expect this Canadianism to start appearing in more and more international dictionaries.

Until now, most referred only to allophone's original meaning as the term for a family of speech sounds heard as the same sound. The word is from Greek, "other sound." "Anglophone" and "francophone" are also coined-for-Canada terms that only recently have made it into international dictionaries. But one of the earliest references to anglophone and francophone is from *Deniker's Races of Man* in 1900: "In Canada two-thirds of the white population are Anglophones and the rest are Francophones."

While anglophone and francophone have been nouns and adjectives in Canada for a century, they only recently entered common usage in other countries. They're now recognized as legitimate English words by lexicographers.

Originally anglophone and francophone simply meant English speaking and French speaking. With Canada's official bilingualism, anglophone, has come to mean an English-speaking inhabitant of a bilingual or multilingual country.

Anglophone derives from the Latin *angli* (the English) and the Greek *phone* (sound, voice).

Similarly, the companion francophone is generally defined now as a French-speaking inhabitant of a bilingual or multilingual country.

The two terms show up in the 1970s in a few lexicons, such as the *Gage Canadian Dictionary* and *Supplement to the Oxford English Dictionary*. By 1986, they appeared in the addenda to *Webster's Third New International Dictionary*.

The K word
Should I say KIL ometre or kil OM etre?

KILometre. That was the word from Canada's former chief of weights and measures, Robert Bruce. The federal metric commission made the same call before disbanding in 1985. Most of the world accents the first syllable. Britons accent the second. They also drive on the wrong side of the road.

Worthy men and women
Why are mayors called Your Worship?

In this sense, worship goes back to its original medieval meaning, worthship — worthiness — rather than reverence, as it later became in the religious context.

The distinction has been around more than eight centuries, ever since the office of maire was introduced in England by Henry II.

The maire (soon spelled major or mayor) administered the affairs of a town and sat as chief magistrate to mete out justice. Magistrates were addressed as Your Worship, just as justices of the peace are now, when on the bench.

The judicial function continued over the centuries and came to early Canada with the office. The Ontario Municipal Act used to define mayors by virtue of their office as justices of the peace.

The office of mayor is no longer defined in the municipal act, confirmed Elaine Ross, a provincial Ministry of Municipal Affairs lawyer, who is working on the act.

But the traditional form of address remains. "Respect for office is often shown in the use of titles and particular forms of address, which impart dignity to the proceedings," noted Michael Smither, publisher of *Municipal World* magazine and author of *Lord Mayor-Lord Provost*. But such titles as Your Worship, Lordship and Honorable "belong to the office, not the incumbent."

Mayors are usually addressed as Mr. Mayor or Madam Mayor in council and other meetings, but also as Your Worship if a speaker happens to be a formal person. Mayors are often misintroduced as Your Honor — the American style for mayor — and the Honorable.

Style books suggest that in correspondence, the envelope should be addressed to: His Worship (or Her Worship)/The Mayor of ... (Informally: His Worship John Smith/Mayor of ...). In formal conversation Sir or Madam is correct. Informally, use Mr. Mayor or Madam Mayor, as the case may be.

Canada also has a Lord Mayor. The distinction, unheard of outside the major cities of the British Isles belongs to Niagara-on-the Lake, Ont. No record of the grant can be found, but that's the way it's been for two centuries. Smither said the belief is it originated with the town's establishment as the first capital of Upper Canada. John Graves Simcoe, the first lieutenant-governor, must have pulled strings back home. Any documentary evidence disappeared when the Americans torched all but one house in the town during the War of 1812.

The Lord Mayor's office said the incumbent is styled Your Worship, not Your Lordship.

Something 30
What is the origin of the traditional "30" at the end of a reporter's copy?
It means "the end." Various sources say it began with Canadian journalists about 1910, using the telegraphers' code in which numbers stood for words or sentences.

Telegraphers used an XXX symbol to designate the end of a long message, especially a story filed by a newspaper correspondent. Reporters substituted the 30 since XXX is 30 in Roman numerals.

Some old newshands still use 30 out of habit when finishing a story written on a computer.

Original Canuck
When did the term Canuck become a word meaning a Canadian?
Canuck (or Canack) originated about 1850 as a derisive term for French Canadians. In England during World War I, it was applied to all Canadians. The etymology of the "uck" or "ack" is obscure, but may have come from Indian word endings.

Incredibly inflammable
How can flammable and inflammable mean the same thing?
Both mean "easily set on fire." Inflammable is more usual in Canada. As you indicate, "in" prefixed to many words gives them a negative meaning. Examples are incapable, inconsiderate and indecisive. But in other cases it can strengthen a meaning.

Millions, billions
When Canadian newspapers report things like the British deficit, do you use the English or American billion?
In Canada and the U.S., a billion is a thousand million (nine zeros). In Britain and most of Europe it's a million million (12 zeros). We convert the bigger billion to the Canadian billion when necessary. Overseas, the billion is called a milliard.

Big numbers
What comes after a trillion? A zillion?

Denominations in the North American system are: million, billion (nine zeroes), trillion (12 zeroes), quadrillion, quintillion, sextillion, septillion, octillion, nonillion, decillion, which has 33 zeroes, and on up and up — but no zillion. A zillion is a large indeterminate number.

In the European system, read million, milliard (9 zeroes), billion (12 zeroes), on up to decillion, which would have 60 zeroes, and on to even higher denominations.

The system used in Canada and the United States was modelled on France's old numbers tables, though the French long ago adopted the British and German system of millions, milliards, billions. ...

Thousands in Ms and Ks
Why are the letters M and K used to mean thousands, as in, "My salary was $30K last year"?

M is the Roman numeral for 1,000. K is the symbol for kilo, a prefix for thousand in the metric system. Kilo comes from *khilioi*, the ancient Greek word for thousand.

Chaos in the House
What does the term filibuster mean?

Centuries ago it described a freebooter — a pirate or military adventurer who fought against another country without authorization of his own government.

Filibuster came into political usage about the mid-1800s. It's mostly used today to describe a parliamentary tactic, usually by minority members of an assembly, to block a bill, create an impression than the majority has lost control, to force an election or any combination of these.

Generally, this is attempted by talking or by reading lists into the record to consume time. Other tactics include ignoring bells for procedural votes and raising point after point of privilege.

It's usually an Opposition tool, but in Canada it's also used by governments to "talk out" Opposition proposals.

The majority may let filibusterers speak till they drop from exhaustion or may invoke closure if rules of the legislature allow. In Canada, closure may be moved in the House of Commons after due notice by a cabinet minister. But there's no closure in the Senate.

The uproar in the Senate in late 1990 over introduction of the goods and services tax had the elements of a classic Canadian filibuster. Among the best-known filibusters in Canada's past are those that occurred during the 1964 flag debate and the 1956 pipeline debate.

Political scrum
What is a scrum and how did it gets its name?
It's a very informal kind of press conference where reporters wait for a newsmaker, surround him or her and fire questions.

Newspapers in Canada and Britain began describing impromptu news conferences as scrums in the early 1970s. Scrum is short for the rugby scrummage (or scrimmage). That's a formation in which crouching forwards lock arms and push against opponents to gain the ball fed into the middle to begin play.

The scene of reporters and photographers surrounding and moving with a newsmaker is not unlike that of a rugby scrummage. There are no rules in a news scrum, though.

16

CANADIAN CORNUCOPIA

Canadian liquor content

Why is Scotch whisky and gin made in Britain, for example, weaker in Canada than in the country of origin? How much weaker? Do all provinces in Canada water down their booze? The Food and Drug Act, which defines standards for all types of spirits, doesn't set a minimum or maximum limit on alcohol content, according to Health Canada, the department that administers this law.

So nothing prohibits lawful sale in Canada of liquor packing the punch of, say, 60 per cent alcohol by volume if that's what most consumers want.

"There is, however, a world-wide standard adopted by most countries — not all, and not all distillers will follow that — of 40 per cent alcohol by volume," said JoAnne Ford, who fielded the question for Health Canada. "So 40 per cent alcohol is what you would see in most liquors."

It's a matter of marketing and/or regional preference, she said. "For instance, if people in certain countries are used to a stronger liquor, (distillers) may sell a stronger liquor there, whereas in Canada they may go with what the average standard is."

Another factor is price. At last check, Canada's excise duty was $11.066 per litre of pure, absolute alcohol. At 40 per cent alcohol by volume, the duty is $4.43, and at 60 per cent, it is $6.64. Higher taxes, plus any mark-up for the stronger drink, reduce its market.

Provincial liquor boards don't "water down" booze. Most of the alcohol is distilled and bottled at the point of manufacture.

Percentage of alcohol is expressed as "proof" and is listed on liquor bottle labels in various countries. The term goes back to sailing days. A proof spirit could burn as a fuel, which was "proof" of its strength. Alcohol wouldn't flame up when watered down to less than 11 parts alcohol by volume to ten parts water.

In the United States, proof is two times the percentage of alcohol. So a bottle of 100 proof liquor in the States is 50 per cent alcohol by volume. In Canada and Britain 100 proof represents 57.1 per cent alcohol by volume.

There's proof that Canadian liquor is quicker than U.S. liquor.

Setting the Canadian table
Is there a unique Canadian food? A friend seems to think it is butter tarts.

Not one, but a cornucopia. Butter tarts, which may have originated with early Scottish settlers, is considered a quintessential Canadian food. Among others are sugar tarts, Nanaimo bars, blueberry grunt (east coast steamed pudding), anything to do with maple syrup, Ontario cheddar, Oka cheese, fiddleheads, wild rice, Arctic char and B.C. smoked salmon.

Quebec's famed *tourtiéres* and way with *poutine* are distinctive, as are Acadian *fricots* (soups consisting of potatoes, meat and fish).

So is bannock, various Canadian-developed grains, McIntosh Red and other apples, Canola oil. ...

That's a partial list whipped up in *The Toronto Star*'s kitchen.

"Native food in the last couple of years is really up and coming," added Theo Lennartz of the George Brown School of Hospitality, the Escoffier Society's Toronto chef of the year in 1992.

Among varied aboriginal dishes are beaver tails in sauce. Ace Toronto chef Jamie Kennedy suggested adding southern Ontario's wild leeks to the list.

He said a growing movement back to regional cooking "is taking advantage of what the summer has to offer, the abundance, and then processing or canning what's left for winter."

Regional cooking was a popular art until shortly after World War II, when tastes turned to imported foods.

Now Canadian cookery has developed a global reputation. The country's top chefs over the past 15 years routinely return with planeloads of medals, gold, silver and bronze from international competitions.

They emerged best in the world at the Culinary Olympics in Frankfurt, Germany, in 1992, beating out renowned chefs from 30 other countries. Their dishes celebrated foods of native people.

In addition, a Canadian team of five aboriginal chefs won seven golds, two silver and two bronze for native *haute cuisine*.

Canadian rye whisky and ice wines are famous world-wide. Domestic red and white wines have started winning gold against the finest vineyards in the world. And not only are Canadian wines gaining respect internationally but, by gosh, at home, as well.

Hangover remedy
What's a prairie oyster?
1. A hangover remedy featuring a raw egg and other ingredients such as Tabasco and Worcestershire sauce.
2. A bull's testicle.

Dinner and supper
Is there a difference between dinner and supper in Canada? Is one term British and the other American, or what is really the proper way to refer to the 6 p.m. meal?
Dinner for centuries was the chief meal of the day, taken at mid-

day, and supper the last meal of the day — as in breakfast, dinner and supper.

Here's an illustrative quotation from *The Oxford English Dictionary* from 1818: "A mechanic ... has three meals a day; coffee with fish or meat for breakfast, a hot dinner; and tea (called supper) in the evening."

That changed for many after the upper crust in 19th century England began to call their evening meals "dinners." In time, "dinner" for fashionable Victorians became a social function, a formal meal of many courses, usually taken in the evening. Supper became their after-theater meal. But not everybody swallowed the toffs' style.

In Canada, dinner and supper are both used in reference to the evening meal, though on social occasions, at least, dinner has a more formal connotation. For others, dinner is still the midday meal.

It really depends on custom or preference: one family might correctly refer to their meals as breakfast, lunch, dinner, and a light supper at bedtime. A neighbor might just as properly call the same meals breakfast, dinner (or lunch, if packed for work or school) supper and bedtime snack.

Dinner and supper, evolving from ancient French words, appear in written English in the 1200s. *Super*, the Old French parent of supper, meant "eat one's evening meal," while dinner meant midday meal.

Depending on where you look, lunch and luncheon evolved either from lump, bunch and hunch (for hunk) or the Spanish *lonja* (slice). Lunch and luncheon appear in writing in the 16th century. Originally a snack between breakfast and the midday meal, lunch became widely used in the 1800s as the term for the noon meal. Today, lunch is the word for the midday meal in the business world, as in "Let's do lunch."

Here's another illustrative quote, from the *Pall Mall Gazette* of 1892: "That period of the evening from 7 to 10 — which in parliamentary phrase is called the 'dinner hour.'"

Since then, at least on social occasions, dinner implies a heavier, more formal evening meal, as in "a black-tie, $200 a plate dinner," and supper usually means a lighter, more festive meal, as in "a gala wedding supper." But a big dinner also can be festive and served at any time noon to night — Christmas dinner, for example.

Confusing? Well, consider that the dinner, like *déjeuner*, goes back to a Latin word that means break a fast.

So the etymological meaning of dinner is breakfast.

Ahhh, salmon
What is the difference between red sockeye salmon and pink salmon?

Both are among five kinds of Pacific salmon ranging along British Columbia's coast. Sockeye, also known as red and blueback, averages less than three kilograms and is canned as choice red salmon. Pink, averaging under two kilograms, is the smallest, most abundant and usually cheapest of the Pacific salmon.

Canadians generally prefer the more intense flavor of sockeye. The milder taste of B.C. pink is usually preferred in parts of Asia and Europe, said Susan Schenkeveld, chief of technical services for the Department of Fisheries and Oceans' inspection branch in Burnaby, B.C.

Pink and sockeye come canned as skinless and boneless salmon, or packed with the skin around the outside and bones, or as salmon flakes or chunks. Pink, which is less firm in texture than sockeye, is not as often sold as fillets, steaks and fresh, head-off, dressed fish.

The three other salmon are spring, also known as chinook; coho and, considered at the bottom in table quality chum.

Corn in fall cornfields
Why are so many fields of corn unharvested by late fall?

That's field corn out there, used for animal feed and for a range of products, including pharmaceuticals. The sweet corn enjoyed at our tables was harvested earlier.

The field corn can be harvested at any time during the fall and winter because it's dry, said Ralph Brown, a biological and agricultural engineering expert at the University of Guelph.

It's harvested when completely mature, which means the seeds have dried right up and are hard. Sweet corn, which we eat, is harvested while it's still in the sugary stage.

"They're two different crops. They look the same but, in fact, they're used quite differently," Brown said.

Pricey peppers
Why do yellow peppers cost more than three times the price of green peppers, and red peppers sometimes twice as much green?

Factors in the steep price difference from yellow to green are longer ripening for red and yellow, transportation costs — particularly air freight from overseas — supply and demand and the lower value of the Canadian dollar against U.S. and European currencies.

Green peppers on Canadian shelves over the summer are mostly domestically grown. Red peppers are mostly imported during the summer from places like California, though some come from B.C. hothouses. The Canadian red pepper harvest brings their prices down in late summer.

But the yellow and orange peppers, longest to ripen and pricey in any season, are flown into Canada from greenhouses in Holland, Belgium and other parts of Europe.

"Air freight, that's why the costs are higher, whereas green peppers are local. That is the most obvious reason," said Tony Fallico, buyer for fruit and vegetable dealer F.G. Lister and Co. at the Ontario Food Terminal in Toronto.

"And anything that's really greenhouse is going to cost you a little more money. They're speciality crops," he said. "You got something everybody wants, you raise the price; if everybody is growing them, the price would be depressed."

"There are some (yellow, field-grown) California peppers, but what we like here is this offshore product. It's much better look-ing, better tasting," he said.

Peter Stonehouse of the Ontario Agriculture College, University of Guelph, an authority on farm economics, said another factor in the price difference has been the low value of the Canadian dollar against European and American currencies.

But it's not unusual to air freight perishable food products here from all over the world. "We have one of the best, most cosmopoli-tan ranges of food available anywhere," Stonehouse said. "It's a mark of our rather high standard of living in terms that we can afford to do this sort of thing."

Melon juice
Why do I never see watermelon juice anywhere? Melons are so juicy.

Sales of watermelon-flavored drinks just didn't go down well in Canada, said executives at two fruit-drink manufacturers.

"There have been watermelon drinks — 25 per cent juice — in Ontario, but they didn't generate enough sales so chain stores delist-ed them. Manufacturers cleared them out," said Peter Mattison, an executive at Sweet Ripe Drinks of Mississauga, Ont.

Mario Allaire of fruit-drink maker A. Lassonde Inc. of Rougement, Que., agreed. They used to produce a Fruite watermelon drink. "It was available. It was a good product. But we had no sales so we discontinued it."

But if you're really thirsting, keep an eye out for any specialty juice stores in your town. They may have fresh, 100 per cent water-melon juice. Or make your own.

A trout by any other name ...
Is there a Canadian fish that sounds like namacush?

Namacush or *namaycush* is an Algonquin name for lake trout.

17

GAMES WE PLAY

A Canadian compromise
Which is Canada's official sport, lacrosse or hockey?
By law, both. Lacrosse became Canada's national summer game and
hockey Canada's national winter game in 1994, in a quintessentially
Canadian compromise.

A private member's bill introduced by Nelson Riis, New Democrat
MP for Kamloops, had named hockey alone as the official sport of
Canada. With the game's soaring popularity in the United States and
overseas, he wanted to ensure its Canadian nature remained intact.
But MPs from all parties insisted on the inclusion of lacrosse, the tra-
ditional native game played long before the first Europeans arrived.

Jesuit missionaries named it *la crosse* because the stick's shape
reminded them of a bishop's staff.

Lacrosse was the country's most popular sport until about 1900,
when hockey ascended. National lacrosse tournaments played a
part in helping unite the unwieldy young nation. It was North
America's first organized sport, with a national governing body and
standardized rules.

The legislation recognizing hockey and lacrosse received royal
assent and came into force on May 12, 1994.

So ended a century of debate. Arguments over which was Canada's national sport — by tradition, numbers of players and fans, endorsements by governors general, etc. — had been going on since the 1890s. In the end, it seems everybody won.

That is the Canadian way.

Also in the Canadian way, nobody really won. Eight months after lacrosse was named an official sport, the Canadian Lacrosse Association learned that Sports Canada was cutting its $190,000 annual funding by 60 percent for 1996 and to zero in 1997.

Hockey scores in the hearts of Canadians
What's Canada's most popular sport?

Samplings in 1991 and 1996 suggest every sport is loved in its season in Canada, but hockey is the national passion in winter.

If you're asking about sports in a recreational sense, though, walking, bicycling and swimming are usually the top three in national fitness surveys.

Jogging or running, skating, cross-country skiing, fishing, tennis and golf are high on the lists, too, along with Alpine skiing.

The number of people in Canada who snapped on Alpine skis at least once a winter or played one game of golf or tennis in summer have been estimated at about four million.

In competitive sports, hockey is the most popular game in virtually every category, from numbers of participants registered (names and addresses, not estimates) public opinion polls, size of television audiences and so on.

Ball — baseball and softball — curling, figure skating, football, golf, soccer, and many other sports are hugely popular, as well. But none makes the heart race like a big hockey game.

Remember the outpouring of national pride when Paul Henderson scored the goal that won the 1972 Soviet-Canada hockey series? That was a defining moment in Canadian sports — the Canadian equivalent of "where were you when U.S. astronauts landed on the moon?" For most Canadians, the answer was watching the game on televisions set up in the factory, office, warehouse, schools or at home.

The size of the national audience for the historic game broadcast on CTV September 28, 1972, is believed to be the largest ever in Canada to watch a sporting event. But in 1972, TV audiences weren't measured daily and none was taken that afternoon.

The known record TV sports audience was 6.7 million who tuned into CTV for the Blue Jays' historic first World Series triumph in 1992. More than three million tuned into the first game of the Toronto Blue Jays–Minnesota Twins American League baseball pennant series in 1991.

But game in and game out, hockey is Number One on television.

CBC-TV's biggest television audiences for a single sports event: 6,192,000 for NHL playoffs, Edmonton Oilers *vs*. New York Islanders, May 19, 1984; 5,724,000 for Team Canada *vs*. Soviet Union, September 23, 1974 (yes, 1974, not the famous '72 series); 5,310,000 for the Oilers–Islanders playoff game on May 17, 1984. Fourth was the Ben Johnson 100-metre final at the Seoul Olympics, September 24, 1988, also watched by more than five million people.

"Going by the ratings, it's still hockey," said Bob MacGregor, a CBC spokesperson.

Also, "Hockey Night in Canada" is a ratings leader, even in weekly competition with regular TV entertainment. Including the top U.S. shows, hockey is the only sport in the top ten most-watched programs during its regular season. The two main regularly televised sports on the Global network are hockey and NFL football, with hockey drawing the biggest audience.

Other sports show big numbers television, though mainly when championships are at stake.

The Canadian Football League's Grey Cup championship generally draws more than three million viewers. More than 3.5 million Canadians per minute watched the Argonauts beat the Calgary Stampeders in the 1991 Grey Cup (a time when the CFL's obituary was already being prepared by sports pundits). And despite wintry winds gusting to 70 km/h, 52,564 fans turned out to Regina's Taylor Field, expanded to twice its capacity, for the 83rd Grey Cup, November 19, 1995, when Baltimore beat Calgary and took the cup to the States for the first time.

Curling draws big audiences as well — about 3.5 million tuned in at some point to the 1995 Brier championship game, with the average per minute at 1.24 million. The women's Tournament of Hearts final had a total reach of 3.3 million.

Figure skating championships also draw television audiences, in the mid-three-million range — an average 1.67 million per quarter hour period for each of the five broadcasts of the 1995 World's and 1.3 million in any quarter-hour period during the Canadian championships.

Stadium crowds: too many variables make stadium audiences difficult to compare among the various sports. For instance, Canada's two big league baseball stadiums hold three or four times the crowds that can fit into the country's seven professional hockey arenas.

Still, on a good summer night 50,000 people watch baseball at the SkyDome while another 25,000 are at Olympic Stadium in Montreal, for a total of 75,000 fans. On a winter night, a total of about 109,000 people attend NHL games in seven Canadian cities.

National polls: a random survey of 1,400 Canadians by sociologist Reginald Bibby of the University of Lethbridge in 1991 found that of the four major professional sports studied, 36 per cent said they closely followed the NHL; 27 per cent chose football (16 per cent favoring the CFL and 11 per cent the American game); 23 per cent went with baseball. About 5 per cent followed the NBA, but that was before the NBA returned to Canada.

The NHL was also the favorite league of young people, as shown in a survey of 4,000 teenagers between the ages of 15 and 19 the following year by Bibby and Toronto-based consultant Don Postererski. About 45 per cent of those polled said they followed the NHL. Baseball was next at 36 per cent; NBA at 29 per cent; NFL,

26 per cent, and CFL, 24 per cent. Their favorite sports star though was Michael Jordan of the Chicago Bulls, just ahead of Wayne Gretzky, then of the Los Angeles Kings.

Registration figures provided by sports associations: 584,783 registered players, coaches and officials in the Canadian Hockey Association in 1995, 513,207 of them players; 483,686 players with the Canadian Soccer Association; 519,000 players, coaches and officials with Baseball Canada, 73,058 of them coaches and officials; 113,067 players with the Canadian Lacrosse Association.

Registration figures don't include many thousands of players in intra-school leagues, or recreational and tyke leagues not registered nationally. For example, the lacrosse association estimates the number of players at more than 200,000 if pupils and students playing in school gym programs are included.

Estimates for softball are about 2.5 million participants, divided equally between men and women, from once-a-year company picnic players to schools and industrial league to interprovincial champions.

The Canadian Curling Association estimates 1,577,000 people play at least once a year, with 502,000 regulars playing at least once a week at the 1,203 facilities across the country. The Canadian Figure Skating Association had 194,914 registered members of all ages in 1995.

Studies for the Royal Canadian Golf Foundation have suggested at least four million men and women play golf at least once a year. The 1,859 facilities in the golf association had about 200,000 members over age 18. These numbers go back to the association's last studies, in 1990.

Athletics Canada's registration includes 25,000 track and field athletes and coaches, 100,000 runners in road racing series and 100,000 youngsters in track and field programs. The figures don't include scores of thousands more not connected with athletic organizations.

Estimates in other sports: more than 700,000 Canadians go

fishing, about 400,000 play squash and more than 300,000 turn up at bowling alleys for ten-pin or the Canadian game of five-pin bowling.

The name of The Game
How did hockey get its name?

Nobody can say for sure. But it seems to have come from hock, an old variation of hook, for the bent shape at the end of the stick. The word's earlier ancestor was probably *hoquet*, Old French for a shepherd's staff, which is crooked at the end.

Games played with bent sticks and balls go back to at least 500 B.C., as shown in ancient Greek bas-reliefs. The first written mention of hockey was as a forbidden game on Sundays, described in the Galway Statutes of 1527 as "… horlinge of the litill balle with hockie sticks or staves." The game has also been spelled hocky, horkey, hawky and hawkey.

In Canada, in the winter of 1867, soldiers of the Royal Canadian Rifles took hockey from grass to ice at Kingston. Various forms of hockey had been played on Canadian ponds before then, according to anecdotal evidence, but the soldiers' ice hockey games became famous. Formal rules were set down for the sport in 1875 by McGill student J.G.A. Creighton in Montreal.

By the late 1800s ice hockey was widely known as a Canadian winter game played on skates with hooked sticks and a puck. By the end of the century it had replaced lacrosse in popularity.

The origin of the word puck for the rubber disk is also obscure. But puck once meant to poke (to hit or strike) in some dialects in Britain and Ireland. Quite likely the verb puck became a noun on Canada's frozen ponds.

Three-wicket hat trick
What's the origin of the hat trick?

Hat tricks have always been part of the magician's repertoire. But the term entered the sports lexicon via cricket more than a century ago. A bowler who took three wickets on three successive balls usually won a new bowler hat from his club or admirers might pass a hat for a collection.

"He thus accomplished the feat known as the 'hat trick' and was warmly applauded" — *Daily Telegraph*, London, 1882. "Mr. Absalom has performed the hat trick twice" — the *Sportsman*, England, 1888.

The term was picked up in hockey and soccer to mean the scoring of three goals in one game by a single player.

Though the cricket connection is obvious, a misconception persists that "hat trick" originated with hockey in Canada.

Toronto hatter Sammy Taft is often credited with giving the term to hockey in the 1930s when he began presenting fedoras to players who'd potted three goals in a game.

Meanwhile, some folks at Henry the Hatter, a century-old Detroit firm, believed the hat trick began there as an early tie-in with the Red Wings. And Biltmore/Stetson Inc. began a tradition of awarding hats to Guelph players performing the feat in the late 1940s.

Another suggestion is it simply arose from hockey fans' practice of joyfully tossing hats on the ice or passing the hat for a collection to reward an amateur hero's third goal of a game — especially when scored consecutively in a single period.

Now that deserves a tip of the hat for sure.

Averaging goalies
How do you figure a hockey goaltender's average?

Divide the number of goals allowed by the number of minutes played and multiply by 60, say hockey writers.

For example, say a goalie appears in 19 games and plays 1,023 minutes (just over 17 complete 60-minute games). And say opponents scored 51 times against him. His goals against average then is 2.99.

Hall of trophies
Where is hockey's Canada Cup kept?

In the Hockey Hall of Fame at the corner of Yonge and Front Streets in Toronto. So are the Stanley Cup, Allan Cup, Memorial Cup and other coveted trophies of the game.

Kurt's quad

Who did the first quad in championship figure skating? Why isn't the back flip allowed in competitive figure skating?

Canada's Kurt Browning, winner of four world championships in men's singles, was the first, performing a quadruple toe loop during the 1988 world championships in Budapest.

He finished sixth that year and won the first of his four world championships in 1989.

Many have completed quads in practice, but only a handful have pulled off the trick in competition, including Elvis Stojko, Canada's latest men's singles world champ, with quads and triples in combination.

The back flip isn't allowed in competition because it is considered to be an acrobatic move and, therefore, illegal.

Garden games

Why is the word "garden" used for sports arenas, such as Maple Leaf Gardens, Boston Garden and Madison Square Garden, when we know that they are not gardens?

Another definition of garden is a large enclosed place where people go for amusement. This might be a hall or arena for sports, such as hockey or basketball, or for circuses and for exhibitions, such as boat and auto shows. Garden comes from an ancient German word, *gart*, meaning enclosure.

Ben's dash

If you converted Ben Johnson's 9.79 time over 100 metres at the Seoul Olympics, how fast would he have been running in kilometres an hour?

Johnson averaged 36.77 km/h (22.85 mph), just under the speed limit on many residential streets, from a standing start in the 100-

metre final at the 1988 Summer Olympic Games in Seoul, South Korea. He was actually clocked at up to 42.37 km/h (26.33 mph) during the race.

But the mark vanished. Johnson had been using a banned steroid. He was barred from competition for two years and the world-record time erased. But in the brief hours the record stood, here's how it compared with the fastest land animals: a cheetah's top recorded speed is 113 km/h (70 mph), a wildebeest, lion or gazelle can reach 80 km/h (50 mph), and a quarterhorse was clocked at up to 76.5 km/h (48 mph).

But Johnson, in effect, outran a charging elephant (40 km/h or 25 mph), and challenged a white-tailed deer (48 km/h or 30 mph).

All in vain.

Athletic émigrés
Why are Canadian citizens able to play on French, Italian and other foreign Olympic teams?
Dual citizenship.

Dart strategy from a champ
Why don't the numbers on the dart board run consecutively clockwise?
The game wouldn't be challenging if all the big numbers were massed in one area of the board.

"The board is laid out in such a fashion that if you go for more points and miss, you will get fewer," said John Part, 27, of Oshawa, the 1994 world champion dart player. "In other words, the 1 and 5 are adjacent to the 20, the 3 and 7 are adjacent to 19."

The middle numbers are closest to each other such as 14 and 11 and 10 and 15. "But you'll never win a game of darts shooting at that because players shooting at the 20 will beat you down," he said.

On second thought, shooting for the middle numbers might not be a bad strategy for beginners, added Part, who defeated the best darters from around the globe to win the Embassy World Professional Darts Championship in England.

Darts have been played at least since the Middle Ages. Foot-long missiles were hurled at log ends of felled elm trees in the 1200s, said Ian Collett of Brampton, a fount of data on dart history. The game became popular and evolved in English pubs during the 19th century, but it was not until the 1940s that the board and other aspects of the game became standardized.

How the Brier got its name
Where did the name Brier originate as the name of the Canadian Curling Championship?

The full name is the Macdonald Brier Tankard and it originated in 1927 with the first Dominion curling championship for men, sponsored by the W.D. Macdonald tobacco company. "The company had a brand of pipe tobacco called Brier. They attached that name to the championship," said Warren Hansen, director of competition for the Canadian Curling Association.

He credited the Brier with creating the impetus that led to the foundation of the association in 1935. "The fact that the Macdonald's Brier got curlers together from across the country raised interest in curling and in the idea of an association," he said.

Twelve rinks, the champion from each province plus Northern Ontario and Yukon-N.W.T., meet annually for one of the most famous trophies in Canadian sport.

CFL's secret weapon
Is the drop kick still alive in Canadian football?

The drop kick is alive and well and living in the Canadian Football League rulebook. The rules still allow the ball to be kicked as it hits the ground.

But the last drop kick occurred about 1982, in a pre-season game. Argos' Jan Carinci drop-kicked a convert.

It was last seen in a regular season game in 1948 at Winnipeg's old Osborne Stadium, Blue Bombers *vs.* Calgary Stampeders.

Winnipeg quarterback Don Hiney was preparing to hold the ball for placekicker Bob Sandberg. A bad snap or a fumble ensued. Hiney picked up the ball and drop-kicked it between the uprights for a field goal.

Go, Roughies!
Why are there two teams in the Canadian Football League with the same name, Rough Riders and Roughriders?

They used to be in different leagues and kept their names when the CFL was formed in 1958. Before then, the Saskatchewan Roughriders played in the Western Interprovincial Football League and the Ottawa Rough Riders in the Interprovincial Rugby Football Union, better known as the Big Four.

The Rough Riders football club, formally organized in 1876, was given the nickname for lumberjacks who rode logs down the Ottawa River. The team became the Ottawa Senators in 1924. The Regina Rugby Club, which formed in 1910, acquired the name Roughriders, for bronco-riding cowboys, in 1924 and kept it when Ottawa switched back to Rough Riders in 1926.

CFL interlocking season games didn't start until 1961 but the two old leagues had met in east-west Grey Cup championship games as far back as 1921. Rough Riders and Roughriders met on the gridiron for the first time in 1951. Rough Riders beat the Roughriders 21-14. It must have been hell for radio broadcasters.

SkyDome sellouts vary
Why do attendance figures vary for sellouts for baseball games at the SkyDome in Toronto?

Sellout figures vary from game to game for two reasons: complimentary tickets are not included in the paid attendance figures and the number of tickets sold to holders of luxury boxes varies.

SkyDome baseball attendance marks were set and surpassed several times each season into the 1994 strike-shortened season.

Take the 1992 season when the Blue Jays became the first major league team ever to reach four million in attendance, breaking a record they set the previous year of 3,885,284 paying customers.

The first mark was 50,211 that April 27; eclipsed by 50,299 on May 28; then 52,383 during the All-Star game on July 9, the biggest baseball crowd to date. But a new mark for regular season games was set by 50,326 fans on July 27. These were among 47 sellouts in 61 home dates.

Complimentary passes aren't issued for All-Star games, so every single spectator was counted as paid. During regular season games, the crowd count goes up or down according to the freebies.

Also, each box holder has to buy a minimum of 16 tickets to Blue Jays games. In theory, the skyboxes are always sold out. But many boxes can hold up to 40 people. When holders buy more tickets for extra guests, as they did for the All-Star game, the paid-attendance count goes up.

For the record, the biggest SkyDome crowd was 73,500 for Billy Graham's Crusade on June 11, 1995. Next was the 67,876 people out for Wrestlemania on April Fool's Day, 1990.

Jays never won a "pennant"

When a major league baseball team wins "the pennant," does it actually win a flag?

The answer is yes and not quite.

The winner of the NL championship series is presented with a pennant. No doubt about it, said the league office and Atlanta Braves who flew theirs along with the World Series championship banner in 1995.

In the American League, "winning the pennant" is just an expression, although symbolically correct.

The AL winner each year gets a trophy and the right to have a championship pennant made and flown at its own expense, if it wishes.

"They have (a championship flag) made and fly it themselves.

It's not provided," said Phyllis Merhige, the league's director of public relations.

They do receive a championship trophy, the William Harridge Trophy, named after a league past president, she said. This is presented to the ownership. Team executives Paul Beeston and Pat Gillick accepted it when the Toronto Blue Jays won the 1992 and 1993 league championship series.

But AL teams do not necessarily hoist a league championship pennant. Take the Minnesota Twins, who won the AL championship in 1991 by beating the Toronto Blue Jays in the playoffs. Rob Anthony, the team's spokesperson, said "What we won was the right to hoist a pennant. In our case, we painted it on the outfield wall — which just says that we were the American League champs."

Over at the Atlanta Braves, Melanie Jesse of the team's media relations staff said the National League Champions pennants flying over Fulton County Stadium in recent years had indeed been presented by the league.

Let's play byesball
When was baseball first played in Canada?

A game resembling modern baseball — though it had four "byes" (bases) along with a home bye — was first played in Beachville, Ont., near Woodstock, on June 4, 1838, a year before Abner Doubleday's mythical game in Cooperstown, N.Y.

The Beachville byesball game, to celebrate the quelling of the Rebellion of 1837, seems to have been the first recorded match between two teams organized specifically to play the game, the first to have nine innings (though seven later became the norm), runs for scoring, three outs an inning, tagging and force outs.

It's called Ford's game after Dr. Adam Ford, a Denver physician, who later described it in detail, in a letter to a U.S. journal, *Sporting Life.*

The teams, Beachville and the Zorras (from the townships of Zorra and North Oxford), were on the field four years before New York businessmen got together to play, eventually forming the Knickerbocker Base Ball Club, considered baseball's first organized team.

Knickerbocker founder, Alexander Cartwright, wrote rules for the game and established the diamond layout in 1845-46. Baseball infields had usually been square before then and runners put out by being hit (called plugging or soaking) by a thrown ball, as in the British game of rounders.

It's known that Doubleday, a U.S. Civil War hero, who'd fired its first shot at Fort Sumter, was at West Point the day he was said to have invented baseball at Cooperstown.

Baseball and cricket may have a common ancestor, an English farm game called stoolball played in the 1300s, in which a batter with his hand or a stick kept a thrown ball from hitting an upturned three-legged milking stool.

Expos' logo
What does the Expos' crest represent?

The National League baseball team's logo is an M for Montreal. The red curl on the left is a lower-case e for Expos and the blue b-shaped curl on the right stands for baseball. The design is intended to symbolize the flow and grace of the game.

Red, white and blue are Montreal's traditional sporting colors, as worn by the Montreal Canadiens hockey team and by the old Alouettes of the Canadian Football League.

Paydays for millionaires
How are Blue Jay baseball players paid — weekly, every two weeks, year-round or only during the season? How much would they bring home on payday?

Ball players pick up their cheques on the first and 15th of every month during the major league season, which runs from April into October.

The field manager and coaches are paid twice a month through-out the calendar year. Some players are also paid over the 12 months if their contracts call for it.

A pay stub, in U.S. funds, might look like this for an American player on a $1 million season contract: the gross is $82,457.65 and, after Canadian and U.S. taxes, nets out at $48,214.33. Deductions for unemployment insurance, U.S. social security, medicare and other odds and ends take away another couple of hundred. The player would take home about $48,000 U.S.

That's based on a 15-day pay period during the baseball season. The net is about $51,200 for a 16-day pay period in months that have 31 days.

Calculating the Canadian and U.S. taxes on the $1 million is rather complicated. But if the income is divided into $500,000 earned in Canada and $500,000 earned in the United States (based on 81 home games and 81 away games, with about 20 off days factored in evenly on both sides of the border), here's how it would work out:

The $500,000 income earned in the U.S. is taxed at 34 percent. The $500,000 U.S. earned in Canada is converted into Canadian funds and taxed at 49 percent. The after-tax Canadian earnings are then reconverted to U.S. dollars since the players are paid in that currency.

Playoff money is paid 30 days after the last game of the World Series. The funds are wired to the club by the office of the commissioner of baseball, and the club cuts a cheque for each member according to the share awarded by a vote of the players.

A ball for fans

How many foul balls do the Toronto Blue Jays or Montreal Expos lose in the stands during an average ball game?
In major league ball parks, the number varies depending on the distance between the foul lines and the stands, but 25 is about average. The Jays put it at 23 to 27 a game.

They're off — counter-clockwise

Foot racing, horse racing, dog racing, cycling, motor racing, ballroom dancing, figure skating, baseball, plus many other moving sports, why do they all go anti-clockwise?

"People are stronger on the right side," said psychologist Ken Hill of St. Mary's University in Halifax, an authority on enviromental psychology. 'The dominant, stronger side is the right. They can push off better on the right side."

So it's simply easier for runners to circle counter-clockwise than clockwise. At least it is for 90 per cent of people. Only about 10 per cent are stronger on their left side, and left-handed.

The counter-clockwise pattern was adopted for other sports because "people just generalized from foot racing," Hill said. "Foot racing is the oldest sport of that sort."

Exceptions arise. Horse races run clockwise on some tracks in Europe and Australia. And many, if not most, racing car circuits, go clockwise.

The first basketball game

Was basketball invented in Canada?

No, the country was the United States. But the inventor was a Canadian, James Naismith (1861-1939), born on a Ramsay Township farm, near Almonte, Ont.

He created the game in December 1891, while a 30-year-old physical education instructor at the International YMCA Training School — now Springfield College — in Springfield, Mass.

The McGill University physical education grad went on to become a medical doctor, chairman of the phys-ed department at the University of Kansas for 40 years, a U.S. citizen at age 64, and would be on hand in 1936 to see his game played as a full Olympic sport. He'd also be credited with inventing the protective helmet for football.

But here's the story of that first basketball game, compiled from files in the athletic department at Springfield College:

Naismith, an outstanding lacrosse and rugby player in Canada, was asked by his department head to devise a team game that could be played indoors in winter.

After some experimentation, he pencilled a set of 13 rules and had them posted on the bulletin board. He asked the school janitor to fetch two 15-inch by 15-inch boxes to be used as "goals."

Then, soccer ball in hand, Naismith assembled his class of 18 young men in the school gymnasium, divided them into two teams and explained his rules.

Meanwhile, the janitor couldn't find boxes of the specified size. He showed up with two half-bushel peach baskets instead. Would they do? They would, Naismith said. The baskets gave the sport its name.

That historic game began with nine men a side on the gym floor. It featured a lot of running and passing (dribbling came later). In the end, only one basket was scored.

Naismith published the rules in the school paper the next month and the new game quickly spread to gymnasiums across the continent. Early basketball courts were often enclosed by wire mesh and that's why players are often called cagers.

Women picked up the game quickly, but men were barred from gyms when they played, a 1893 Springfield newspaper clipping shows. Women played in their bloomers.

Professional leagues started up before the turn of the century. An exhibition game was played at the 1904 Olympics. In 1912, an unknown genius cut the bottom out of the nets.

Short for motor sport
Is Mosport named for motor sport or after former racing driver Stirling Moss?
The name of Mosport Park at Bowmanville, Ont., is a contraction of motor sport.

18

RADIO TO SCTV

Call signs for radio stations
Why do all radio station call letters start with a C? How are broadcasting stations assigned call letters?

As a member of the International Telecommunications Union, Canada is given a block of call signs for use in this country. Under ITU agreement, signs for broadcasting stations in this country start with the letter C.

In the U.S., it's W east of the Mississippi River and K west of it, with blocks assigned from WA to WZZ and KA to KZZ.

Call signs beginning with the letters CF, CH, CI, CJ and CK are reserved for broadcasting in Canada. These first two letters are followed by two more, for a basic four-letter call sign.

"We maintain a list of call signs, which is available to prospective broadcasters, and they select the one they like," said Steve Burak of Industry Canada's Spectrum Management, which used to be Communications Canada.

By special arrangement, stations owned by the Canadian Broadcasting Corp. may have call signs beginning with CB, as in CBLT in Metro. And three-letter call signs may be assigned to national networks, such as CTV.

The Global Network's call sign is CIII, but announcers use the company name, Global.

The suffixes FM and TV are used to identify frequency modulation radio and television stations.

The department's Broadcast Rules and Procedures forbid assigning a proposed call sign to a station when there'd be a phonetic spelling similarity with another station's letters within a 300-kilometre (186-mile) radius, or any overlap in their service areas.

Royalties from radio

When a radio station plays records, do they have to pay royalties? How much, and how does the copyright work?

The radio stations pay royalties to song writers and music publishers, but — at the time of writing — not to the performing artists or the recording company.

It works this way. A commercial music radio station pays 3.2 per cent of its gross revenues to SOCAN, the Society of Composers, Authors and Music Publishers of Canada. This money, totalling more than $21 million, is pooled.

The composers and music publishers in Canada and abroad share revenues from the pool according to SOCAN's monitoring of frequency of play of their tunes across the country. This is a representative sampling of radio station logs based on music format, geographic region and language, said Paul Spurgeon, SOCAN's general counsel.

The more a piece appears on the logs, the larger the royalties the copyright holders will receive.

But two other elements are in this entertainment equation — recording artists and record companies/producers. Under the old rules, they didn't get a cent, said Brian Robertson, president of the Canadian Recording Industry Association.

For example, Gordon Lightfoot would get royalties as a composer for his hit songs aired on radio globally, but not as the singer of those hits. Céline Dion, who doesn't compose her songs, would get no royalties from radio for the thousands of hours of air play of her voice in Canada and around the world.

That's because Canada and the U.S. were not among the 90 countries of the world that have performers' rights protection for artists and record companies. While they're not, there's no reciprocity from countries where these royalties are paid.

Changes proposed to the Copyright Act of Canada, called "Neighboring Rights" would allow both the performing artist and the recording company to receive compensation when a radio station plays a recording, Robertson said. "We anticipate they will become law in 1996."

So the money Canadian and U.S. artists make come not from songs played on radio, but from from record sales and concerts. Unless, of course, they've composed the hits aired.

Why Channel 1 vanished
Why don't we have a channel 1 on television sets?

Blame the Americans. Our giant cousins dominate the airwaves and made the rules before TV came to Canada.

The old channel 1 had been tuned out by the time the first television stations opened in Canada in 1952 (CBFT in Montreal on September 6 and Toronto's CBLT on September 8).

In fact, regular television programming was introduced in the United States on channel 1, with RCA's W2XBS telecast of the opening ceremonies of the New York World's Fair on April 30, 1939.

What happened to that channel, along with channels 14 to 19 on the Very High Frequency (VHF) television dial, is a long and fascinating story, described in technical detail in the March 1982, issue of *Radio-Electronics* magazine.

In a nutshell, the frequencies that had been assigned to channel 1 — 44 to 50 megahertz (MHz) — were reassigned to fixed and mobile services, such as emergency and business two-way communications, by the Federal Communications Commission in the United States in June 1948. The FCC decided not to re-number the channels when adopting standards for television broadcasting at that time.

Channel 1 had been bounced around to different bands during television's experimental years. These had begun in earnest in 1933 when RCA demonstrated the first successful all-electronic television service, from its experimental transmitter, W2XBS, at the top of the Empire State Building in New York City on the 44 to 50 MHz band — channel 1.

In 1940, channel 1 and the other channels were moved up the spectrum and Channel 1's original band was given to the newly developed Frequency Modulation (FM) broadcasting.

But by 1945, the number of television channels on the VHF spectrum was reduced to 13 because of interference on the spectrum and the need to fit in new communications requirements growing out of technology developed during World War II. The FM dial was then assigned what is now the 88-108 MHz slot and Channel 1 went back on the 44 to 50 MHz band.

Meanwhile, the FCC was seeking frequencies for fixed and mobile communications and, to make room for them, finally tuned channel 1 out permanently in 1948.

TV and cable channels
Why do TV stations have different channels on cable than they do on antenna?

Broadcasters want to protect the picture and sound quality.

The channel change ensures there's no interference from the local broadcaster's transmitter when you're watching that station on cable TV, said Alan Leung, head of regional broadcast engineering for Spectrum Management's Toronto office.

"If you used the same channel on cable, the TV would pick up both the cable and the on-air signal" he said. "The signal sent through the broadcaster's transmitter could leak into the cable system and you'd get interference."

Pay for TV infomercials
Are the people making testimonials on TV infomercials paid for that?

"Of course. Absolutely," said Mark Locher of Los Angeles, who took our call as national spokesman for the Screen Actors Guild.

"It's just like a commercial, and the actor gets paid like any commercial."

But what if the infomercial is a non-union production? Locher said the question covered an area outside his jurisdiction — Screen Actors Guild members cannot appear in a non-union production.

But, he added, "Nobody does these things for any reason except to make money. That's the whole point. Everybody is paid quite well in those."

In Canada, pay for testimonials on infomercials, known in the trade as "industrial shows," is covered by collective agreement with the Alliance of Canadian Cinema, Television and Radio Artists.

Along with scale for an actor with, say, one line on a half-hour industrial show in Canada, are "use patterns"—residuals that depend on such factors as the size of the viewing market and number of weeks the program's aired.

Celebrities appearing as hosts or narrators command fees many times scale. If the star owns an interest in the goods or services advertised, income from sales generated by the infomercial could be far more lucrative than an appearance fee.

The Canadian Radio-television and Telecommunications Commission (CRTC) deems infomercials to be commercial advertising material, which is limited to 12 minutes per hour during the regular 18-hour broadcasting day. That's why infomercials air only in the wee hours on Canadian stations.

Movie runs in Canada
How do Cineplex Odeon and Famous Players decide who gets which movies in their theaters?

"The exhibitors don't decide which movies they're going to play. It's the studios who decide where they want to put their films," said Howard Lichtman, executive vice-president of marketing for Cineplex Odeon.

Historic relationships between studios and exhibitors generally determine where films play. But, particularly in Canada, "nothing is etched in stone and it's not black and white," Lichtman said.

For example, Paramount owns Famous Players. At the time we called Lichtman, the Paramount hit, *Lassie*, was being screened at Famous Players theatres but it was also showing at Cineplex Odeon's Canada Square in Toronto. "This is one small example. I could show you the reverse," he said.

Fifth estate
Why is the TV show called the *fifth estate*?

The name refers to the power of television. "The genesis of the idea was if print was the fourth estate, then electronic journalism was the 'fifth estate'," said Peter Herrndorf, chairman of TVOntario, who'd headed CBC-TV current affairs when *fifth estate* was born in the 1970s.

The first three estates from the Middle Ages were the clergy, nobility and commoners. The press became known as the "fourth estate" in 19th century Britain because of its growing power and influence.

A debate at the CBC about who came up with *fifth estate* has never been settled. Herrndorf mentioned two versions.

Glenn Sarty, the program's first executive producer, had played with a list of names and started a staff contest that generated names from three dozen people. "Glenn to this day feels it was the name he brought forward."

Another version suggests two independnt producers some time before had submitted a proposal for a documentary on electronic journalism entitled *Fifth Estate*.

Measuring TV audiences

How are sizes of audiences for television shows measured in Canada? How do television stations know what I'm watching?

Two methods are used by Nielsen Marketing Research in Canada: the "People Meter" to measure national audiences, and a viewers' diary in selected communities to gauge local preferences.

The People Meter is a monitor that sits on top of every television set in 1,500 homes across Canada — one of the homes has eight TVs. Ages, income ranges and other demographic information for each member of a volunteer household are compiled.

Each person has a number with which to log on to a meter whenever they decide to watch television or log off when they've got something else to do.

"All of the channel changes are metered automatically so that our meter knows what channel viewers are watching, whether it's cable, off-air or through the VCR," said Michael Leahy, media marketing manager for Nielsen.

Daily, in the wee hours between 3 a.m. and 6 a.m., the information contained in the meters is downloaded into the company's computers in Markham and processed. Weekly reports are published on audience sizes for various programs across Canada, projected from the sample findings.

The householders are not paid except for expenses directly related to the sampling, such as telephone charges. They'll participate in the survey for about two years though some may be sampled for up to five years.

The diary method involves a booklet randomly distributed to homes in selected communities across the country. Householders fill in demographic information and then, over three weeks, note who's been watching what each day. Canada is "swept" in March and November to determine television audience choices in specific markets.

Fictional Anne
When was *Anne of Green Gables* published? Was it based on the author's life?

Anne of Green Gables, Lucy Maud Montgomery's first novel was published in 1908. The best-selling series set in Prince Edward Island about a spirited orphan who found a home with an elderly pair was not autobiographical, but did draw on her girlhood experiences in P.E.I.

Montgomery's *Emily* trilogy is said to be autobiographical.

Emergency exits
On the main floor at Roy Thomson Hall, why are there no red exit signs above the doors? Every other public hall and theater I've seen has them.

You had officials who first fielded the question wondering about it themselves. Staff even checked records and regulations all the way back to the architectural designs.

Then Susan Jegins, vice-president of operations at Roy Thomson Hall, got back into town and provided the answer: The floor has continental seating — center aisles — and on either side of each row of chairs is an exit door, so it complies with Ontario fire regulations, she said.

Red exit signs are clearly visible at exits in corridors, as well as in the mezzanine and balcony floors, where you have to walk upstairs to reach doors.

Cinema's 50-foot kiss
Who were the actors in the first screen kiss?

A Canadian comedienne, May Irwin (1862-1938), and actor John C. Rice made screen history when they locked lips in a famous 1896 flick, *The Kiss*, showing the kissing scene from their New York stage play, *The Widow Jones*.

The brief film, shot at inventor Thomas A. Edison's studio in Orange, N.J., was billed as "The 50-Foot Kiss" and "The First

Shocker." It was. Audiences were stunned; clergymen raged at the immorality, and the press called it "absolutely disgusting."

This outcry troubled Irwin who began her career as Georgina Campbell in a church choir in her hometown of Whitby, Ont. She always maintained she never sang a risqué song or spoke an off-color line. The Broadway star made only one other movie, the four-reeler *Mrs. Black is Back* in 1914. But her close-up kiss assured her a place in film history.

Art of the tax break
Do Canadian corporations get any tax breaks for buying Canadian art?
A Canadian work of art is considered a corporate asset to earn income. A firm may defer taxes by claiming a 20 per cent depreciation allowance annually, even if it's appreciating in value. If it sells the work, the company is taxed on its original price plus any profit.

Badge of honor
What were the lapel pins worn by "Front Page Challenge" panelists Betty Kennedy, Pierre Berton, Jack Webster and, when he appeared on the show, Knowlton Nash?
Their Order of Canada pins. The CBC television panel show was broadcast from 1957 until it was cancelled in 1995.

So long, gang
When did The Happy Gang last perform?
They reunited for two concerts at the Canadian National Exhibition in 1975, 16 years after their long reign on CBC Radio ended.

Laugh a minute
How many shows did SCTV produce?
The equivalent of 185 half-hour shows now syndicated in Canada, although some were hour-long.

19

DEBT AND TAXES

A family deep in the hole
What's the federal government's debt load?
In round figures, the government's revenues run about $130 billion a year, but it'll spend maybe $32 billion more than it takes in this year. The national debt is about $578.4 billion. On the plus side, the Gross Domestic Product is in the $780 billion range.

Put it this way, if the Canadian government was a family netting a well-to-do $50,000 a year, it would be spending $62,300 a year, $12,300 more than it earns.

It would have total assets of about $300,000 — the house, car, furnishings, collectibles, RRSPs, a few investments.

But its total debt would be about $225,500. Interest charges on the debt would be about $18,000 a year. It would have to borrow to pay the interest.

At its rate of spending — even if most of the $225,500 debt is the mortgage on their main asset, a house — that "family" is in big trouble.

Back in 1990, when it was spending $12,000 a year more than it was earning and owed $160,000, we asked chartered accountant Cyril Sapiro, a trustee specializing in personal bankruptcies, what advice he'd give them. "Cut back, pay off the debts and cut your foolish spending," he said.

Good advice.

Pay in the good old days

My pay in 1957 was $65 a week. How much would that be today? Is there a formula for converting old amounts to today's dollars?

That $65 paycheque in 1957 would be worth $385.67 in current dollars. The intervening years of inflation and growth accounts for the difference.

On the other hand, $65 now would be worth about $10.96 in 1957 dollars.

To compare the purchasing power of a dollar then and now, you have to use the Consumer Price Index for both years. Statistics Canada's CPI number for 1995 was 133.5. It was 22.5 in 1957.

To determine what $65 then would buy now, divide the 1957 price index (22.5) into the current price index (133.5) to get the growth rate over the years, and multiply that by $65. The answer is $385.67.

To find out what $65 now would buy then, divide the current CPI, 133.5, into the CPI for 1957, 22.5, and multiply by $65. The $10.96 represents the amount inflation has shrunk the purchasing power of $65 over the intervening years.

Here are the price indexes at five-year intervals in the past: 1920, 17.3; 1925, 13.9; 1930, 13.9; 1935, 11.1; 1940, 12.2; 1945, 13.9; 1950, 19.0; 1955, 21.5; 1960, 23.7; 1965, 25.7; 1970, 31.0; 1975, 44.2; 1980, 67.2; 1985, 96.0; 1966 (the base year), 100; 1990, 119.5.

So how much was your first paycheque and how much could it buy today?

Last federal surplus: 1970

When is the last time a Canadian government had a budget surplus?

The federal government under Liberal Pierre Trudeau had a surplus of $332 million as of March 31, 1970. The national debt — accumulated federal deficits since Confederation — totalled $16.9 billion at the time. Interest costs were $1.7 billion.

By 1982, the debt reached $100.6. The cost of servicing it came to $15.1 billion.

As of March 31, 1996, the net debt stood at about $578.4 billion. Interest charges were about $40 billion.

Before placing all the blame on today's politicians, remember Joe Clark. Voters in the 1980 federal election cast out his minority Conservative government largely over its attempt to balance the budget through a gasoline tax of four cents a litre. The national debt at the time stood at $72.2 billion.

Taxman around the world
Where does Canada stand among countries that pay the highest amount of taxes?

In terms of total tax revenues expressed as a percentage of Gross Domestic Product (GDP), Canada ranks fifth in personal income taxes and 15th in total taxes among the world's 24 most highly industrialized nations.

Personal income taxes in Canada, federal and provincial, amounted to 13.5 per cent of the GDP, the value of all goods and services produced in the country during the year. That followed Denmark's 26 per cent, Sweden's 18.4 per cent, New Zealand's 16 per cent, and Belgium's 13.9 per cent.

By comparison it was 10.2 per cent in the U.S. and 9.3 per cent in the United Kingdom and 7.5 per cent in Japan. In Greece it was only 3.6 per cent.

The figures are from a study between 1985 and 1993 by the Paris-based Organization for Economic Co-operation and Development.

Total taxes include sales taxes, property taxes, taxes on corporate profits and social security contributions, as well income taxes. In Canada, this amounted to 35.6 per cent of the GDP.

Total tax burdens were heaviest in Denmark and Sweden at 49.9 per cent of GDP; followed by the Netherlands at 48 per cent; and

Norway and Belgium and Finland, all at 45.7 per cent. Also ranked ahead of Canada were Luxembourg at 44.6 per cent of GDP, France (43.9 per cent), Italy (43.8), Austria (43.6), Greece (41.2), Germany (39), Ireland (36.3), New Zealand (35.7).

Among the countries below Canada on the list were the U.S. at 29.7 per cent and Japan at 29.1 per cent.

The Canadian numbers include the impact of the goods and services tax, introduced in 1991 to replace the hidden manufacturers' sales tax. Canada was also in 15th place in total tax revenues in 1990.

And while Canada has a lower total tax burden than many other countries — the OECD average was 38.5 per cent — that's because contributions toward social security are lower than in most European countries.

In 1993, social security contributions amounted to 5.9 per cent of GDP. In France, it was 19.1 per cent, 18.3 per cent in the Netherlands and 16.3 per cent in Belgium, where such contributions were highest. Germany's was 15.1 per cent. U.S. contributions were also higher, at 8.7 per cent. In Japan, they were 9.8 per cent. The OECD average was 10 per cent. When social security contributions are excluded, Canada rises to ninth place in term of taxation.

Michael Walker, head of the Fraser Institute, a conservative think-tank in Vancouver, said that other countries have faced the fact their populations are aging and require increased contributions to pension plans. Canada has not yet adjusted to this, he said.

In terms of taxes on corporate profits, Canada was in the lower third at 2 per cent. The OECD average was 2.6 per cent, from a high of 7.2 per cent in Luxembourg, 4.3 per cent in Japan, and 4.1 per cent in Italy to a low of 0.9 per cent in Iceland, 1.1 per cent in Turkey, 1.2 per cent in Finland and 1.4 per cent in Germany.

Other comparisons: in the U.S., taxes on corporate taxes were at 2.3 per cent, United Kingdom 2.4 per cent, Japan 4.1 per cent. But France took less from corporations than Canada, 1.5 per cent.

Of course, corporations paid municipal taxes, as well. For all Canadians, revenues from property taxes represented 4 per cent of

GDP, or 11.1 per cent of total taxes, highest of the 24 countries in the OECD study. The OECD average was 2.1 per cent of GDP and 5.7 per cent of total taxes.

Canadians, detesting the GST and provincial sales taxes, might be surprised to learn that though taxes on goods and services represented 26.6 per cent of total tax revenues, this was among the lowest in the study. Only Japan, 14.4 per cent, U.S., 17.2 and Switzerland, 16.7 were lower. The OECD average was 30.1 per cent.

Sales taxes in Canada amounted to 9.5 per cent of GDP. The OECD average was 11.6 per cent.

Deficit and debt
What's the difference between the federal deficit and the national debt?

A deficit is the amount federal spending exceeds revenues in the government's fiscal year. The debt is accumulated deficits, the amount expenditures have exceeded revenues since Confederation.

A $32.7 billion deficit for the 1995-96 fiscal year increased the debt to $578.4 billion.

$110 billion owed abroad
How much of Canada's national debt is owed to foreigners?

At last check, $110.4 billion was held by "non-residents" — offshore individuals, corporations and financial institutions.

The total national debt includes the "unmatured debt," all the money the government owes on the financial markets, and "unmarketable debt," mostly money the government has borrowed from its employees' pension plans.

That $110.4 billion in foreign holdings represented about 25 percent of the unmatured debt, according to the finance department's Debt Operations Report issued in December 1995. That reckoning dealt with the 1994-1995 fiscal year. When all numbers were in, the national debt stood at $545.7 billion, including the unmatured portion of $441 billion.

The unmatured debt in financial markets — not the money the government owes on its own accounts — is the part of the debt that influences the value of the dollar and interest rates when bond holders and buyers get nervous.

Here's how the unmatured debt pie gets sliced in rounded figures: marketable bonds in Canadian currency, $225.7 billion; Treasury Bills, $164.5 billion; Canadian Savings Bonds, $30.5 billion; marketable bonds in foreign currency, plus Canada Bills (treasury bills in U.S. currency), $16.9 billion and, under other, $3.5 billion.

On top of that was the unmarketable debt of $109.2 billion, most of it — just over $101 billion from monies borrowed from government employee pension plans. This does not include $32.7 billion in current liabilities, such as $18.4 billion held in accounts payable (owed for goods and services, tax rebates and the like), money held in interest and debt accounts for such things as uncashed Canada Savings Bonds, interest coupons, and $4.8 billion held in interest and debt accounts for such things as uncashed Canada Savings Bonds, interest coupons, and so on.

All this adds up to minus $582.9 billion. This is offset by $37.2 billion in assets, including $5.1 billion in cash reserves and $14.4 billion in foreign exchange accounts. And that's how the $545.7 billion federal debt added up in 1995.

Free at last
What is "tax freedom day" in Canada?
Tax freedom day is a term used by the Fraser Institute, for the theoretical day in the year when the average Canadian family has earned enough to pay all taxes imposed by all levels of government.

From that day, in effect, "the average Canadian family starts working for itself," says Michael Walker, the institute's executive director.

Tax freedom day in 1995 ranged from June 5 in Newfoundland and June 9 in Nova Scotia to July 16 in Ontario and July 18 in Quebec.

"The Fraser Institute's calculations for tax freedom day for every province really comes up with what the tax burden feels like for a typical family. But there the issue becomes a little clouded," said David Perry, head of research at the Canadian Tax Foundation.

That's because average family incomes from each province are thrown into the pot, mixing those in high-income provinces such as British Columbia and Ontario where the averages may be $55,000 to $65,000 a year with those in Prince Edward Island at $35,000 to $40,000 a year.

"The taxes paid by these families will be quite different," Perry said. "For one thing (in B.C. and Ontario), you're further up the progressive income tax schedule and decisions to buy heavily taxed goods are going to change with family circumstance."

That said, here are the tax rates as a percentage of cash income for families, as provided by the Fraser Institute for 1995: Prince Edward Island, 38.3 per cent; Nova Scotia, 41.6 per cent; New Brunswick, 37.6 per cent; Quebec, 42.5 per cent; Ontario, 46.5 per cent; Manitoba, 45.5 per cent; Saskatchewan, 44.3 per cent; Alberta, 47.3 per cent; British Columbia, 47.6 per cent.

Taxes in times past
How did the federal government raise money before the income tax and sales tax were instituted?

Customs duties on imports mostly, and a bit from excise duties on things like tobacco and alcohol, said Peter DeVries, director of the fiscal policy division for the federal finance department.

Federal income tax and corporation taxes were introduced in 1917 to finance Canada's role in World War I. Federal sales taxes, including the manufacturers' sales tax, now replaced by the GST, followed in 1920. Government didn't need much in the nation's first 50 years, obviously. The federal government collected $212 million in the 1916-17 fiscal year.

Of that, $134 million was from customs duties, $28 million in excise duties, about $12.5 million in "excess profits" tax on corporations, about $33 million in miscellaneous receipts, and a few million from crown corporation earnings.

For comparison, the federal government expected to collect from all sources about $133.2 billion in the 1995-96 fiscal year, about $30 billion less than projected expenditures. About $114 billion is for program spending and all the other costs of running Canada, and $49.5 billion is made up of public debt charges.

The bottom line: the federal government of the '90s spends more in a day than the $212 million collected in an entire year back in 1916-17.

Quebec's top trading partners

How much trade is there between Quebec and the other provinces and with the rest of the world?

Quebec sells more goods and services to the other provinces of Canada than it exports to the rest of the world, interprovincial trade figures show.

Quebec also enjoys a trade surplus within Canada. It has a balance of trade deficit with the rest of the world.

Ontario is an even bigger winner in interprovincial trade, but it also imports more from other nations than it exports.

Those were among the findings of Statistics Canada studies on interprovincial trade between 1984 and 1989, completed a couple of years ago.

The StatsCan figures were echoed by a joint study by the Canadian and Quebec chambers of commerce that found Quebec had a $1.1 billion trade surplus with other provinces in 1993.

For the last year of the StatsCan study, the flow of goods and services from Quebec to other provinces totalled $34.7 billion, and $22 billion of that went to Ontario.

The flow of commodities from other provinces to the Quebec market — including $25.7 billion worth from Ontario — reached $32.9 billion. The net result for Quebec was an interprovincial trade surplus of $1.8 billion.

Meanwhile, Quebec's total exports abroad that year amounted to $29.5 billion. Its imports from abroad totalled $35.4 billion, for a trade deficit of almost $6 billion.

For comparison, Ontario "exported" $60.9 billion worth of goods and services to the rest of Canada, thanks in large part to its huge transportation sector — cars, trucks, trains, etc. Meanwhile, "imports" from other provinces totalled $39.2 billion.

Ontario did more trade internationally, but also had a deficit here. Exports abroad totalled $75.4 billion and imports amounted to $83.9 billion.

Trade among provinces in Canada was worth $144.8 billion.

"That's a lot of money and a lot of jobs," said James Nightingale, a research economist with StatsCan's Input-Output Division, which conducted the study.

The chambers of commerce study determined that about 470,000 jobs in Quebec depend on exports to the rest of the country. Multiply that by four to get an approximate figure on jobs across Canada that depend on interprovincial trade. Quebec holds almost a quarter of Canada's population.

In foreign trade, StatsCan found exports from all provinces and territories totalled $159.8 billion in the last year of the study. Imports amounted to $161.8 billion.

As a rule of thumb, about 80 per cent of Canada's international trade is with the U.S.

Tax break in Alberta
Why doesn't Alberta have a provincial sales tax?
It has a nest egg called the Alberta Heritage Savings Trust Fund, from wealth generated by its oil and gas resources in the boom years following the fund's creation in 1976. Financial assets in 1996 totalled about $11.9 billion.

That was expected to provide about $1.02 billion of income to the province.

The fund's contributions to budgetary revenues is equivalent to the revenue that would be generated by a 5 per cent sales tax, the Alberta Treasurer's office has said.

Alberta is the only province that doesn't have a provincial sales tax. The Northwest Territories and Yukon don't have territorial sales taxes either.

Provincial sales taxes in the rest of the country: British Columbia, 6 per cent; Manitoba, 7 per cent; Saskatchewan and Ontario, 8 per cent; Quebec 8 per cent (general) and 4 per cent (services and immovable property); Prince Edward Island, 10 per cent; Nova Scotia and New Brunswick, 11 per cent, and Newfoundland, 12 per cent.

The federal goods and services tax is 7 per cent in every corner of Canada. But the GST and PST will total 15 per cent in Nova Scotia, New Brunswick and Newfoundland from April 1997, under a controversial integration of sales taxes.

Taxes swallow bottle

When I buy a bottle of liquor — rye, scotch or vodka — how much tax am I paying? How much tax am I paying on a bottle of wine?

It varies from province to province but, in general, say you picked up an $21.50 bottle of Canadian whisky at an Ontario liquor board outlet. Of that, $4.37 goes to the supplier, including 4 cents freight, and $17.13 goes to the provincial and federal governments. On a $6.40 bottle of domestic table wine, $2.28 goes to the supplier and $4.12 to governments.

Here's how the liquor board breaks down the tax on the 750 mL bottle of liquor: $3.32 goes for the federal excise tax, $10.07 for the provincial mark-up (for wages, benefits, overheads, profit for the treasury), 22 cents for the provincial bottle levy (which is 29 cents a litre) and 9 cents for the provincial environment fee. That leaves a basic price of $18.07.

On that is the $1.25 for the federal goods and services tax, which is 7 per cent of the basic price, and $2.17 for the provincial retail sales tax, which is 12 per cent of the basic price of a bottle of liquor. So $4.58 goes to the Government of Canada and $12.55 to the Government of Ontario. And, as mentioned, $4.33 to the supplier. On the 750 mL bottle of wine, $2.28 goes to the supplier, 38 cents for the federal excise tax, $1.27 on the provincial mark-up, $1.13 for the provincial wine levy, 22 cents for the provincial bottle levy and 9 cents for the provincial environment fee.

That leaves a basic price of $5.37. The GST is 38 cents and the provincial retail sales tax is 65 cents. That totals $6.40. So $2.28 goes to the supplier, 76 cents goes to the Government of Canada and $3.36 to the Government of Ontario. Cheers.

GDP vs *GNP*

What's the difference between Gross National Product (GNP) and the Gross Domestic Product (GDP), which statisticians now seem to be using?

They're virtually the same. Both refer to the total market value of all goods and services, including wages, produced by a nation over a specific period, usually a year. This is a measure of a nation's economic activity.

Here's the difference: the GDP calculates the value of production in Canada, regardless of ownership of the factors involved in the production. In other words. if a U.S. company has a factory in Canada, its activity would be included in our GDP apart from investment income sent to the U.S.

The GNP calculates economic activity of Canadian-owned factors of production, regardless of where it takes place. In other words, if a Canadian company has a factory in the U.S., profits returned to Canada are included in the GNP.

Most industrial countries use it, though the U.S. still calculates its national production by the GNP method.

StatsCan switched in 1986 to GDP because it relates more closely to domestic prices and employment than the GNP, as well as to provincial employment and economic bookkeeping.

The GDP also conforms to the international practice of

calculating national production as recommended in the U.N. System of National Accounts.

In 1985, investment income received from non-residents was about $8 billion and investment income paid to non-residents was about $22 billion, so the GDP was $14 billion larger than the GNP. In total that year, the GDP was $478 billion and the GNP was $464 billion.

To make it all perfectly clear: "To move from GDP to GNP, add the investment income received from non-residents and deduct the investment income paid to non-residents," Statistics Canada says.

GST costs $369 million
What's the cost of administering the GST?

The cost to the Government of Canada of collecting the GST zoomed to a high of $369,223,000 in the 1994-1995 fiscal year, Revenue Canada figures show. More than a quarter of that was spent to blend Quebec's sales tax with the GST.

Most of the money, $232,621,000, went to salaries and benefits for 5,206 GST-collecting federal civil servants, including those at the new processing center at Summerside, P.E.I. Add $40,632,000 for personnel operations — training, accommodations, telecommunications, travel, and so on.

A one-time $94,495,000 went to the Quebec revenue ministry as "compensation and start-up" to underwrite the province's merging of the provincial sales tax with the GST. An additional $1,475,000 was on the books as "capital."

For comparison, it cost $85,800,000 to administer the old manufacturers' sales tax in the year before it was replaced by the GST on January 1, 1991. The manufacturers' sales tax netted $17.7 billion in 1990. The GST has yet to match that.

In fact, the GST nets less than half of what it collects. The year the $369 million was spent to collect the federal sales tax, it netted $15.578 billion. But the gross amount collected was almost $20 billion more — $35.460 billion.

The other $20 billion went in GST refunds, rebates, tax credits and repayment for government internal transactions.

The bulk, $16.195 billion, was paid out in refunds related to input tax credits, with about 10 percent of that going to municipalities and hospitals. The GST isn't applied only at the retail level. It's like a value-added tax, applied at each stage at which a product is sold, from raw materials, manufacturing, wholesaling and retail. But the GST is refunded at each level prior to the final purchaser.

About $2.816 billion was paid in quarterly tax credits to low-income earners, and $871 million in internal government transactions — one ministry paying another. The government isn't taxed but pays GST and repays itself.

The GST netted $61.7 billion in the first four years after replacing the old manufacturers' sales tax on January 1, 1991, an average of just over $15 billion a year.

The Conservative government of Brian Mulroney was sure it had designed a cash cow. No one foresaw the average Canadian's passionate dislike of the sales tax, which manifests itself as consumer sales resistance, the idea being, if you don't buy, you don't have to pay GST.

Many retailers blame the GST for sluggish sales since 1991.

Exempt from the GST
Who's exempt from paying the goods and services tax?

The only people personally exempt are the governor general of Canada and Indians on reserves or ordering goods (big-ticket items, not pizzas) to be delivered to reserves, says Revenue Canada.

The wife of the governor general would be exempt in making purchases for an official function for him, say, a new outfit for a party to greet foreign VIPs. But she'd pay the tax on the same dress if it had been bought for a private function.

Provincial government departments — but not their people — are exempt from the GST. Federal departments pay the tax, then claim full refunds from the federal purse.

Purchases for the offices of MPs are exempt. But MPs, including cabinet ministers, must pay the tax for all other goods and services they buy.

Foreign diplomats pay GST, but can claim full refunds. Tourists, foreign sports clubs and theatrical troupes can claim refunds on accommodations and meals, but not for ordinary purchases.

That's it. Not even the prime minister is exempt.

GST and foreign tattoos

If I go to the United States and get a tattoo, do I have to pay GST on it when I come back across the border?

Yes, says Canada Customs and Excise. "If it's a service you obtained in the United States that you will enjoy in Canada, technically there'd be a charge," said Donald LaBelle, chief spokesman for the department in Ottawa.

You'd have to remember to declare it, and show a customs officer a receipt before you'd be liable to pay the goods and services tax.

It's the same if you declared a haircut obtained abroad or brought in items that are not subject to duty. The GST legally has to be charged at the border, just as if the goods or services had been purchased in Canada, on amounts that exceed your legal exemptions from duty charges.

Say you were out of the country for at least 24 hours (which entitles you to bring back $50 worth of goods duty-free) when you obtained the tattoo, got a haircut and bought a souvenir, spending a total of $60. The GST would apply on the amount of purchases above $50, or in the case of the tattoo, haircut and souvenir, on the remaining $10.

We're not making this up.

U.S. customs in Canada

Why are there U.S. customs inspectors on Canadian soil? What are they doing at Pearson International Airport departure?

American customs and immigration services have been at Toronto's

Pearson International Airport for about 30 years under a bilateral agreement between Canada and the United States.

Don't knock it. "It's a service to Canadians going into the United States," said Paul Elliott, Revenue Canada's manager of customs passenger operations. "It clears them quicker. If, for instance, they're going into an airport such as Miami, which has a tremendous amount of customs activity, you could be lined up a long time. But if you're pre-cleared, you go right through (domestic areas)."

Pre-clearance of Canadian passengers also helps ease congestion at heavily used U.S. airports, where travellers from abroad may be tied up for hours in customs and immigration lines, he said.

Canada could station customs and immigrations officers at U.S. airports if it wished, but so far has chosen not to. "Whether it's costs, I'm not sure," Elliott said.

Double duty
What's the penalty if a cross-border shopper fails to declare goods purchased in the U.S.?
It depends on the situation. The penalty could run to the seizure of the goods to double the duty and taxes you'd normally pay.

Customs is especially tough on cigarette smugglers. If caught smuggling, say, ten cartons of cigarettes in a hidden compartment in a car, the vehicle could be seized. Penalties under an amendment to the Canada Customs Act raise the maximum penalty for the smuggling of commercial quantities of cigarettes to $200,000 in fines or two years in jail, or both.

RSP or RRSP? RSVP
What is the difference between an RSP and an RRSP?
An extra R. RSP means Retirement Savings Plan and RRSP is Registered Retirement Savings Plan. Whether called an RSP or RRSP, it's a government-approved plan to save money for retirement years — specified contributions are tax-deductible, and the interest is tax sheltered.

20

ODDS AND END

Keep right
Why do Canadians seem to be alone among Commonwealth nations in driving on the right?

Files from the Canadian Automobile Association show Quebecers and Prairie pioneers had always kept right, long before the motor car came along. British Columbia, New Brunswick, Nova Scotia and Prince Edward Islands moved right from the British way between 1922 and 1924. Newfoundland came over in 1947.

Sleigh crashes probably had something to do with it in Ontario. The keep-right rule of the road was established in 1812 by an Upper Canada statute that referred to the passing of horse-drawn sleighs in winter. That was 23 years before England made driving on the left the law.

Using the right side of the road made sense in early work-a-day Canada and in the United States. Most people led work horses and oxen with their right hand. And the heavy animals couldn't nudge them into roadside walls and ditches.

Horses are mounted on the left, so postillions in charge of horses pulling big transports sat on the left side of the tandems.

The riders' left legs stuck out and, unless the transport kept right, could catch against walls or branches.

In Europe, the custom of riding on the left was almost universal up to Napoleonic times. The reasons were different, but made sense from an upper class point of view. A rider on the left side of the road could more easily draw and use his sword if an oncoming stranger had robbery or mayhem in mind. Also, while moving along the left side, a carriage driver's right whip hand was unobstructed by roadside obstacles. Farm and commercial wagons kept left to keep out of the way of the oncoming upper classes mounted or in carriages.

Napoleon came along and changed all that across Europe. But first Robespierre, the revolutionary and atheist, decreed French traffic would keep right, apparently to weaken papal influence over people's everyday lives. Popes had made keeping left mandatory so pilgrims wouldn't wander all over the road.

Napoleon's armies marched across Europe on the right side of roads. Wherever they went over almost two decades, oncoming traffic moved to the right to keep out of their path. And stayed right.

But Napoleon never reached Britain. It stayed left. Scotland made driving on the left the law in 1772, England and Wales in 1835.

Among about 40 countries that drive on the left are Australia, Barbados, Britain, India, Jamaica, Japan, Pakistan, South Africa, Trinidad and Tobago and New Zealand.

Why a quiz?
Why do most contests except government lotteries ask skill-testing questions?

To keep the sponsors out of court. Unless specifically exempted under Criminal Code provisions, they might be charged with running an illegal game of chance.

If the winner of a lucky draw also demonstrates a skill — at arithmetic, say — it's not a prohibited lottery.

Kipling's rings
Why do engineers wear iron rings?

The rings (sometimes stainless steel these days) are supposed to symbolize both humility and pride in building. They are presented during "The Ritual of the Calling of an Engineer," which dates back to 1925 and Rudyard Kipling.

England's first Nobel prize winner in literature devised the rite for the Engineering Institute of Canada, which oversees it through a Corporation of the Seven Wardens.

Some U.S. universities have imitated it but, according to the University of Toronto's Faculty of Applied Science and Engineering, "only Canadian engineers may legitimately wear them."

Lost in the bush
Do people lost in the woods walk in circles clockwise or counterclockwise?

"The environment determines the direction people go," said environmental psychologist Ken Hill of St. Mary's University in Halifax, whose expertise is used by search and rescue organizations.

Some old research suggested that people favor their dominant side when they're lost — right dominant circling counterclockwise and vice-versa for lefties — but there's no good evidence to support that, Hill said.

"There's no condition where the environment is so flat and level that (left- or right-side dominance) would determine the direction."

Original SIN
When did Social Insurance Numbers begin?
1964.

Significant digit
Is there any significance to the first few SIN digits?

Only the first digit has special significance. It indicates the region of Canada from which the application for the Social Insurance Number originally came, said Claude Paquette of the Department of Human Resources in Ottawa.

The numeral 1 signifies it came from the Atlantic provinces; 2 is for Quebec, with 3 in reserve; 4 for Ontario, and the 5 held in reserve was first issued in the fall of 1993; 6 for the Prairie provinces and Northwest Territories, and 7 for British Columbia and Yukon Territory.

A 9, first issued for refugees in 1976, now indicates the application came from a resident who is not a Canadian citizen or landed immigrant.

If that person becomes a citizen, a new Social Insurance Number is issued, with the first number then indicating the region, Paquette said. Citizens keep their numbers for life.

Winning photos
Why do photos of big lottery winners always show them holding their cheques at the bottom left-hand corner?
That's where winners' addresses are printed on lottery cheques. The position of the fingers hides the address.

Why buses lack seat belts
Why aren't seat belts required in buses, especially school buses?
Federal and provincial transportation officials say school buses are probably safer without them. They cite statistics indicating a child is 16 times safer in a bus than belted into the family car. Ontario kids take about 143 million bus trips a year. On average, 200 are bruised but only six to eight require even an overnight stay in hospital.

Why? Buses are sturdier and designed so that passengers aren't hurled through a windshield, against a dashboard or out a door.

In those built since 1980, seats are closer to one another, with better anchoring and higher, padded backs. Transport Canada collision tests using dummies showed that belts could cause more severe head and neck injuries.

Some private schools use older buses, but government officials say their safety records are no worse. As for public transit buses, an additional argument against belts is the nuisance of adjusting one for a short ride, then unbuckling to let others in and out. Inter-urban buses also have high, padded seats and impressive safety records.

True north
Is there an easy way to find Polaris, the North Star?
Ancient mariners located north by drawing an imaginary line up through the two "pointer" stars at the front of the Big Dipper and looking along it to the first bright star — that's Polaris — about three times the distance between the two "pointers."

Changes C to F and back again
What's the formula to convert Celsius to Fahrenheit, and vice versa?
An easy way to convert Celsius to Fahrenheit: double the Celsius temperature, deduct 10 per cent and add 32.

Example: say, it's minus 7 Celsius outside: -7C times two is -14. Deduct -1.4 and you get -12.6. Add 32. You get 19.4 or, rounded off, 19 Fahrenheit.

To find the Celsius temperature from Fahrenheit, deduct 32, add 10 per cent and divide by two. Example: 82F minus 32 is 50. Add 5 and get 55. Divide by two and get 27.5 or, rounded off, 28C.

Joyeux Noel
When was Christmas first celebrated in Canada?
The first Christmas was celebrated by Jacques Cartier and his crew in 1535, at Strathcona, Que.

Thanksgiving began in Arctic
What is the source of the Canadian Thanksgiving Day and why is the date of the celebration different from that in the U.S.?
Americans didn't invent Thanksgiving. It began in Canada. The first recorded Thanksgiving observance in North America took place in

1578 in Canada's eastern Arctic during Martin Frobisher's search for the Northwest Passage. That was 43 years before the Pilgrims gave thanks in 1621 for the bounty that ended a year of hardships and death.

Nova Scotians began observing Thanksgiving Day in the style of their New England neighbors in 1750. United Empire Loyalists later introduced it to the rest of Canada. Dates of the celebration varied as it spread from region to region in both Canada and the U.S.

Abraham Lincoln established the date for the U.S. as the last Thursday in November. In 1941, U.S. Congress set the national holiday as the fourth Thursday in November. In Canada, it was usually observed on the third Monday in October. In 1957, Parliament set the second Monday in October as Thanksgiving Day.

The Canadian holiday draws on European harvest festivals, religious observances in thanking God for plentiful crops, Frobisher and early colonists giving thanks for safe passage, as well as Pilgrim celebrations in the U.S. that began the tradition of turkeys, pumpkin pies and gatherings of families and friends.

Lady Valentine
Who was the Toronto woman who received anonymous valentines for years?
Her name was Meryl Dunsmore. She received the first card when she was 17 in 1928, and the last after she died in July 1988.

That last valentine from the secret admirer for 60 years accompanied a bouquet of flowers at her funeral. It said simply, "Rest in Peace, my Valentine."

Need a vacation?
How many weeks of paid vacation should someone get after being with a firm for five years, and after ten years?
The law does not set out a schedule of vacations for long-time employees. That's between the employer and worker or, in a union shop, determined in collective bargaining.

Canada's Bureau of Labor Information says vacation time varies widely. Of 1,200 collective agreements surveyed in the private and public sectors, 14 per cent provided three weeks paid vacation after five years' service. About 18 per cent of the agreements provided four weeks after ten years' service, 3.7 per cent provided four weeks after five years.

Ontario's Employment Standards Act stipulates an employee is entitled to two weeks paid vacation after one year of service. Vacation pay must be at least 4 per cent of the total wages for the year for which the vacation is given.

The employer decides when the vacation may be taken, but it must be within ten months after the employee has earned it. The vacation may be taken in a two-week stretch or divided into two one-week segments.

Long odds
What are the chances of winning the Lotto 6/49 jackpot?

Odds are 1 in 13,983,816. Odds of getting all seven winning numbers on one line in Lotto Super 7 are 1 in 62,891,499. Lottery corporations advertise these odds at 1 in 20,963,833 for a $2 play of three lines. Chances of being struck by lightning, 1 in about 2 million.

Castles cost a lot these days
How much would Toronto's famous Casa Loma cost to build today?

The last estimate was $41,691,730, broken down into $36,327,260 for Sir Henry Pellatt's magnificent castle overlooking Toronto and $5,364,470 for its fabulous stables. Casa Loma is Spanish for "house on the hill," the name on the deed when Sir Henry bought the property.

Sir Henry, a flamboyant financier worth about $17 million in an era when Canadian workers' wages averaged just over a buck a day, poured $3.5 million into Casa Loma. It took more than three years, from 1911 to 1914, to build and about 40 servants to maintain.

The $41,691,730 total is a replacement cost, taken from an insurance appraisal dated July 31, 1992, said Erlinda Bala, property manager at the city of Toronto property department. The city owns Casa Loma, which overlooks Toronto above Spadina.

A heartbroken Sir Henry, wiped out by financial setbacks climaxed by the collapse of a bank, turned it over to the city in 1924 for back taxes. The landmark has been one of Toronto's great tourist attractions since 1936, operated and managed for the city by the Kiwanis Club.

Body parts and transplants
How do I leave my body parts and organs for transplants? Is it enough to fill out the form on my driver's licence?

Fill out the consent form on your driver's licence and let your next of kin know of your wishes. Although the form is a legal document under the Human Tissue Gift Act, the organs won't be retrieved without the permission of next of kin.

For further information, contact the Multiple Organ Retrieval and Exchange (M.O.R.E.) program at the address or phone numbers that come with drivers' licences.

Canada–U.S. mail flow
How much mail flows back and forth between Canada and the United States?

Canadians, individuals and businesses, receive about 29 million kilograms (64 million pounds) of mail a year from the United States, about 30 per cent of its total foreign mail, figures from Canada Post's international relations offices show.

Canadians send about six million kilos (13 million pounds) of mail there, about two-thirds of Canada's mail to the world.

The figures do not include private-sector courier service volumes.

Getting off mailing lists
Where do I write to get off charities' direct mailing lists?

Write to the Canadian Direct Marketing Association (CDMA), the organization you'd contact to have your name and address erased from commercial direct mailing lists.

Most major charities belong to the CDMA. "With our code of ethics, they must, among other things, take your name off the list on request ... and they must participate in our mediation and arbitration services if there's a problem afterward," said John Gustavson, the association's president.

The address is: The Canadian Direct Marketing Association, Mail Performance Service, 1 Concorde Gate, Suite 607, Don Mills, Ont., M3C 3N6.

Charities and businesses are generally happy to oblige. It costs them plenty in postage to reach every address on their mailing lists. It's money ill-spent on householders they know are going to junk their appeals and advertising unopened.

Trucking on Sundays

What's the status of the operation of trucks on highways on Sundays? I understand that only trucks carrying perishables and livestock were permitted, but I see an increasing number of trucks on the highways on Sundays.

The trucking industry has been free to go about its business on the nation's highways on Sundays for the past decade, after prohibitions on Sunday highway operations were declared unconstitutional by the Supreme Court of Canada.

After passage in 1906 of the Lord's Day Act, a federal statute, trucks were only allowed to operate on Sundays if they carried perishable goods, such as food, medical supplies and cargo considered vital. The act prohibited commerce and labor deemed unessential on the Sabbath.

In the early 1970s, courts often dismissed charges of illegal Sunday operating against truckers carrying general cargo in interprovincial transit, ruling this represented a work of necessity for the public good.

Long-haul firms argued that they should be placed on the same terms as trains and boats, which were allowed to move freight on Sundays.

In 1974, the Canadian Transport Commission began granting inter-provincial firms permission to operate long-haul services on Sunday, saying denial of the applications could have condemned the long-distance trucking industry to "at best an uncertain future and at worst an early demise."

But the trucking industry in general continued to be blocked by the Lord's Day Act. Battles on behalf of short- and long-haul firms continued for another dozen years until the Supreme Court's ruling overturned the prohibitions.

A bestseller in Canada

How many copies of a book need to be sold for it to be considered a bestseller in Canada? How much would the author make?
"It's conventional wisdom that it's 6,000 copies for a small literary work, perhaps a work of poetry or a small writing talent, certainly not the big busters, Mordecai Richler and so on," said Steve Payne, editor of *The Canadian Bookseller* magazine, organ of the Canadian Booksellers Association.

Publishers interviewed said 5,000 or 6,000 hardcover sales would represent a successful book in Canada. For mass-market paperbacks, the numbers rise to 30,000 or 40,000 copies. Sales of more than 10,000 copies of a trade paperback (large-format softcover) will make editors and publishers smile.

But publishers say a perception of a bestseller in Canada is any book that gets on a bestseller list, and sales figures don't always seem to figure in.

Ranking in sales at book stores randomly surveyed across Canada, rather than absolute numbers sold, is often the basis for bestseller lists.

The usual royalty for authors is about 10 per cent for hardcover and 8 per cent for paperback.

For a $30 hardcover book, they would make $3 per book. If it sells 6,000 copies, that's $18,000 for the author at 10 per cent of the gross. For a paperback selling 40,000 copies at $6.95 each, the author's royalty at 8 per cent would be $22,240.

That might be for two or three years' work. They're the lucky ones. Major publishing houses in Canada receive about 3,000 unsolicited manuscripts a year. Maybe three might appear among the 30 or 40 titles published.

INDEX